"I've lost count of the number of books I've read on the Holy Spirit. I've even written a few myself. After a while they all start to sound the same, and I lose interest. Trust me when I say that this will most assuredly not happen to you on reading Jonathan Dodson's excellent book *Here in Spirit*. It is a surprisingly fresh, exquisitely written, biblically rooted, and experientially honest presentation of the Spirit of God as a person with whom we commune right here, right now. Dodson doesn't avoid the controversial elements in the Spirit's work, but that isn't his focus. His aim is to help us grow in our relationship with the Spirit and to open our eyes and hearts to the multifaceted ministries of the third person of the Godhead. I can't recommend this book too highly."

Sam Storms, Bridgeway Church, Oklahoma City

"Warm, pastoral, and filled with scriptural truth and wisdom, *Here in Spirit* reintroduces us to the Holy Spirit so that we come to love him as a person and depend ever more on his power."

Trevin Wax, Bible and reference publisher at LifeWay Christian Resources, author of *This Is Our Time*

"As its name suggests, *Here in Spirit* is a thoughtful discussion of why Christians should not only live in the moment, but in the Spirit as well. Each chapter unveils another revelation of what the Father wants for and from the followers of his Son and why his Spirit is key to it all. Well organized and illustrated, Dodson has gifted the church with a user-friendly pneumatology (doctrine of the Holy Spirit) that seeks to motivate church members to grow in their understanding and experience of the third member of the Holy Trinity. An important book; I heartily recommend it!"

Gary Tyra, professor of biblical and practical theology, Vanguard University

"In *Here in Spirit*, Jonathan Dodson invites us to look up from the usual squabbles over the role of the Holy Spirit, and drink in a grander, richer view of the third person of the Trinity. From the cosmic span of the Spirit who sustains all creation, to his involvement in the ordinary rhythms of our daily lives, this book offers us a deep and yet readable account, which invites us not just to learn about the Spirit but to fall deeper in love with him."

Mark Sayers, senior leader at Red Church, Melbourne, author of *Strange Days* and *Disappearing Church*

"As a trusted guide, Jonathan helps us recover the beauty of a life lived with the Spirit of God inside us. This book will remind you to see God around every corner."

Jennie Allen, author of *Nothing to Prove,* founder and visionary of the IF:Gathering

"Jonathan Dodson's voice is one I trust, and he has written a helpful resource for anyone seeking to understand and know the Holy Spirit. The Spirit has confused Christians on all ends of the theological spectrum, but this book helps us see the Holy Spirit as he's unpacked in Scripture. As the title states, he creates, sustains, and transforms—and we have access to him! I highly recommend this book!"

Matt Carter, pastor of preaching and vision at the Austin Stone Community Church

"John Stott began every day from his waking moment with a prayer to each person of the Holy Trinity, specifically greeting the Holy Spirit and asking him to go on growing his fruit in John's life. And God answered that prayer abundantly! This book would commend such practice, with its strong call to know the Spirit of God in much more personal and intimate terms than before. I am grateful for Jonathan Dodson's challenge. His book is very easy to read, but not at all just an easy read. I have been reminded of things I'd forgotten and rebuked for things I've neglected. The book has blessed my life this very day and will impact the sermon I have to preach in ten days' time. That's because it is resonant with multiple scriptures, rich in honest, personal experience, and constantly relevant to everyday life."

Christopher J. H. Wright, Langham Partnership, author of *Knowing the Holy Spirit Through the Old Testament* and *Cultivating the Fruit of the Spirit*

"Too often, we Christians are content settling for weak, anemic, and un-compelling versions of what is meant to be a strong, healthy, and life-giving expression of life in Christ. Jonathan does a great job drawing us into this more robust, Spirit-led vision for what life can be in the here and now. God has given us an inner resource to help us be and become the very best version of ourselves. It's time we started drawing on that resource!"

Scott Sauls, senior pastor of Christ Presbyterian Church, author of *From Weakness to Strength*

here
in spirit

knowing the Spirit who creates,
sustains, and transforms everything

JONATHAN K. DODSON

IVP Books
An imprint of InterVarsity Press
Downers Grove, Illinois

InterVarsity Press
P.O. Box 1400, Downers Grove, IL 60515-1426
ivpress.com
email@ivpress.com

InterVarsity Press® is the book-publishing division of InterVarsity Christian Fellowship/USA®, a movement of students and faculty active on campus at hundreds of universities, colleges, and schools of nursing in the United States of America, and a member movement of the International Fellowship of Evangelical Students. For information about local and regional activities, visit intervarsity.org.

Scripture quotations, unless otherwise noted, are from The Holy Bible, English Standard Version, copyright © 2001 by Crossway Bibles, a division of Good News Publishers. Used by permission. All rights reserved.

While any stories in this book are true, some names and identifying information may have been changed to protect the privacy of individuals.

Published in association with the literary agent Don Gates of The Gates Group, www.the-gates-group.com.

Cover design: David Fassett
Interior design: Jeanna Wiggins
Images: Portland satellite photo: © FrankRamspott / iStockphoto
textured paper: © ke77kz / iStock / Getty Images Plus

ISBN 978-0-8308-4544-6 (print)
ISBN 978-0-8308-7398-2 (digital)

Printed in the United States of America ∞

InterVarsity Press is committed to ecological stewardship and to the conservation of natural resources in all our operations. This book was printed using sustainably sourced paper.

Library of Congress Cataloging-in-Publication Data

Names: Dodson, Jonathan K., author.

Title: Here in spirit : knowing the spirit who creates, sustains, and transforms everything / Jonathan K. Dodson.

Description: Downers Grove, IL : InterVarsity Press, [2018] | Includes bibliographical references and index.

Identifiers: LCCN 2018017980 (print) | LCCN 2018025654 (ebook) | ISBN 9780830873982 (eBook) | ISBN 9780830845446 (print) | ISBN 9780830873982 (digital)

Subjects: LCSH: Holy Spirit.

Classification: LCC BT121.3 (ebook) | LCC BT121.3 .D64 2018 (print) | DDC 231/.3--dc23

LC record available at https://lccn.loc.gov/2018017980

P 25 24 23 22 21 20 19 18 17 16 15 14 13 12 11 10 9 8 7 6 5 4 3 2 1

Y 38 37 36 35 34 33 32 31 30 29 28 27 26 25 24 23 22 21 20 19 18

Dedicated to professors Richard Lovelace and Colin Gunton,

who taught me to know and enjoy all three persons

of the Trinity.

Contents

The Greatest Gift

WHEN I STEPPED onto the premises of the East Austin projects, I sensed a heaviness in the air. We were serving the community alongside another Christian group. Their group made the initial connection with project residents. Our group provided food and drinks and joined them in ministry. We were eager to lighten the atmosphere there with the hope of Christ. As time passed, the residents began to look forward to our visits. The youth loved connecting with the Christian hip-hop artists who came with us. I had several significant conversations with some of the residents and got to pray for them on the spot. The weight seemed to be lifting.

One afternoon I heard shouting and decided to follow the noise. The ruckus led me to a few residents surrounded by several Christians from the other group, who were praying loudly asking God to baptize them in the Spirit and to give them financial prosperity. I hung back, observed, and prayed. Afterward, one of the people from this group asked me if I was "Spirit filled." I thought to myself, *It depends on the day—or the moment*. But I knew that wasn't what she meant.

So I replied, "What do you mean by Spirit filled?" They responded by describing a person who has had a very specific experience, marked by speaking in tongues. I had in mind the passage in Ephesians where the filling of the Spirit results in singing, thanksgiving, and submitting to one another (Eph 5:18-21). We clearly had two different perspectives of "Spirit filled." Although we both affirmed the miraculous work of the Holy Spirit, our differences became so great we had to part ways. Sadly, our differing doctrines of the Holy Spirit divided us, not just in theory but in ministry among marginalized people. The parting was done in humility and love on both sides, but I left brokenhearted. Does it have to be this way?

Perhaps you've had a similar experience. Or maybe you've been on one side of the divide staring skeptically across the aisle. Or possibly you're in the middle scratching your head. What's so divisive about the "Spirit of unity" (Eph 4:3)?

SPIRIT OF DIVISION OR UNITY?

The Holy Spirit. Three words couldn't divide the church more. I suppose "I hate you" is up there, but that's more of a division between people rather than churches. Entire swaths of Christianity have divided over the third *person* of the Trinity. This division, over the place of the Spirit in the Trinity, left the Eastern Church (Orthodox) on one side and the Western Church (Roman) on the other, which, among other factors, eventually led to what was called the Great Schism.

Doctrine does divide. Attempting to forge unity, I've heard some people say, "Doctrine doesn't matter." Typically, they mean if we would all lay down our doctrines and just focus on Jesus, we would all get along. But that assertion is also doctrinal. It's saying to everyone else, if you lay down what you hold dear, and believe in the Jesus-only doctrine I consider precious, then we can all get along. This approach is well meaning but exclusivist, privileging its own view. It also leaves out the Father and the Spirit. We need to dig deeper. Why does doctrine over the Holy Spirit divide?

The fault line of division over the Spirit today is quite different from that of the early Church. The "great schism" affecting most of the modern church is over the *gifts* rather than the *person* of the Spirit. The division falls rather neatly along just a few of the Spirit's more effusive gifts, things like speaking in tongues, prophecy, healings, and miracles. To simplify it for the moment, there are *charismatics* who treasure and practice these gifts, and *cessationists* who adamantly insist most of these gifts are no longer in effect. The groups shore up, take sides, and accuse one another of wary extremes. Some remain in the middle, self-described "open-but-cautious." Entire denominations, seminaries, and churches divide over their views of these gifts of the Spirit.

Wherever you fall in this debate, I think there's a deeper issue at stake. It's interesting that we don't divide over spiritual gifts like service and mercy. We don't part company over whether mercy is still in effect or if service is still valid. And there aren't too many divisions over faith, hope, and love, what Paul called "the higher gifts" (1 Cor 12:31). Everyone believes in those. Maybe, just maybe, we're fighting over the wrong gifts. Certainly, there are things worth debating. Paul opposed Peter for his gospel-compromising racism. But what is the greater issue at stake here? Quibbling over a few of the Spirit's choice gifts, we've missed the most important gift of all—*the Holy Spirit himself.*

Pigeonholing the Spirit based on a few of his gifts is like sizing someone up after a single conversation. I'm not a big Quentin

Tarantino fan. His films are too violent for me. I've seen clips here and there, and at the behest of several friends I did watch *Inglorious Basterds*. I'll admit the initial interrogation scene is riveting, but I still find the flippant ultraviolence deplorable. So my initial impression of Tarantino was not positive, but that was before I met him in person.

> Quibbling over a few of the Spirit's choice gifts, we've missed the most important gift of all—*the Holy Spirit himself.*

One afternoon as my wife and I were waiting to be seated in a hole-in-the-wall Mexican restaurant, I glanced over the hostess's shoulder. Recognizing a guy sitting by himself in the bar, my wife turned to me and said, "Honey, I think we were in college ministry with that guy." I smirked and said, "Honey, that's Quentin Tarantino." Lunch was dominated by debate over whether we would introduce ourselves to Tarantino after we were done. My wife won the debate, so we walked over to say hi.

To my surprise, Tarantino was quite affable. He asked our names. My wife made a quip about having a guy's name, and when Tarantino heard her name is Robie, he leaned in. He asked how she got the name. As Robie told the story, Tarantino tracked the plot, asked questions, and laughed along the way with two complete strangers. After a bit more chit-chat, he invited us to stay for a drink. We gratefully declined, but I walked away shocked by how kind and inviting he was. Based on his filmography, I figured he'd be a total jerk. If I'd stuck with my initial impression of Tarantino, I would have been wildly wrong.

Sizing the Holy Spirit up based on a few of his gifts is a big mistake. If we relate to the Spirit primarily regarding miraculous gifts, and whether they are operative today, we distort and limit our understanding of the third person of the Trinity. He should be known for much more. Who is the Spirit? Is he a person or a spiritual force? How are we meant to relate to him? Can we pray to the Spirit? Can we worship the Spirit? What is his role in creation? Is he present in culture? What will he do in the future? And what does being filled with the Spirit look like after all? These are some of the questions I'd like to explore. Instead of relating narrowly to the Holy Spirit, I'd like to broaden our engagement with him by touring aspects of his vast character that are often unexplored. In focusing more on *who* the Spirit is, we may find ourselves less divided.

HERE IN SPIRIT

I don't want you to read this book simply to avoid division or handle it more winsomely, although that would be great. Motivation for knowing the Spirit should be much grander. And here it is—*the most meaningful, creative, satisfying life possible is one lived here in Spirit.* The key values of meaning, creativity, and satisfaction correspond to a primary aspect of our humanity—mind, body, and spirit. The Spirit enables us to thrive as whole persons.

> The Spirit enables us to thrive as whole persons.

The mind longs for meaning, coherence, and understanding. When we look up at the stars, we wonder who made them and where we came from. Do we have a purpose in life? Logically, when we balance the checkbook, we expect the math to add up. Philosophically, we ponder what it means to live well. We want to make sense of the world. At some level, we want what's *true*. We value meaning, but we're also not just brains on sticks. We like to make stuff.

Early in life we feel the impulse to create. All three of my children loved to color when they were young. When finished with their thirty-second masterpiece, they would hand it to me and insist I hang it on the wall. As my daughter Ellie grew older, she took to adult coloring books. With precision, and a flair for unique color combinations, she creates brilliant versions of these stock images.

Once when Ellie had finished coloring a wolf, her sister Rosamund blurted out, "Ooh, it's half wolf, half creation wolf." What did she mean by "half creation wolf"? That half of the wolf was marked by a sequence of alternating yet wild and brilliant colors—yellows, reds, and turquoise. The other half of the wolf was filled in with more predictable colors and looked more realistic. Rosamund identified Ellie's creative impulse to expand on the realistic wolf as an act of *creation*.

Rosamund was on to what J. R. R. Tolkien describes as "sub-creation." He writes:

> Man, sub-creator, the refracted Light
> through whom is splintered from a single White. . . .
> The right has not decayed.
> We make still by the law in which we're made.

As subcreators, our impulse to create is a refraction of the great light of God. Every human being is imbued with a desire to fashion because we are fashioned by a Creator who creates with his own two hands, the Spirit and the Son. We desire *beauty*. But creative expression and intellectual exploration alone do not bring ultimate satisfaction.

Deep down we long for something that transcends our own thoughts and cultural expression. We want to be satisfied. I've had nearly flawless days touring ancient ruins on the Wild Atlantic Way of the Irish coast or taking in some of the finest of the art in the world in Paris, accompanied by my favorite person in the world. Yet I still felt dissatisfied at the end of the day. What is that thing that's so difficult to find? Transcendence.

We want to be connected to something greater than ourselves. It's why we adore beauty, climb mountains, and explore religion. In fact, our search for satisfaction can be so intense it dislocates us from the present. Socializing with others, we may half listen to them while scrolling our device for fans, friends, followers, anyone who will pay attention *to us*. Alternatively, we may eject from the present to be connected with world events, up to date with the cultural or global moment. Twitter highlights these for us in a column called "Moments." But alas, our digital search for transcendence often leaves us disembodied in the present, unable to value the person in front of us or enjoy the moment fully.

I've invited several secular friends, along with some Christian friends, to join us for dinner once a week to explore some of life's deepest questions. In advance I encouraged my Christian friends to see this as an opportunity to learn from secular people and value them. One evening we were in the kitchen huddled around the potluck spread on our granite island. I looked up to see one of the Christians I'd invited entranced by his screen, while one of our secular friends stood idly beside him, for quite a while.

In our search for transcendence, we may be "here" but not in Spirit. Cadavers of disembodied yearning, we are "there," seeking satisfaction somewhere in the digital landscape.

Think of the last time you were "caught up in the moment"—singing along in a concert, playing with your kids, laughing with friends, making love. A real, embodied joy. Sociologist Peter Berger describes this experience as a "signal of transcendence." Joy, he says, signals the existence of a transcendent, all-satisfying reality.

The psalmist directs our search to the love of God, "Satisfy us in the morning with your steadfast love, that we may rejoice and be glad all our days" (Ps 90:14). He knows that true joy and satisfaction are found in God. The Trinity—Father, Son, and Holy Spirit—are uniquely positioned to satiate that longing *for all our days*. Unlike any other deity, they experience ongoing self-satisfaction and joy within their perfect community. They give what they have. Feuding gods or lone deities are unable to offer what they cannot experience, interpersonal joy and eternal love within a perfect, divine community. But the Spirit is described as the Father's love "poured into our hearts" (Rom 5:5). He sweeps us up into the fountain of his divine love to bring about true human satisfaction. This is the *summum bonum*, the highest good—to enjoy God in his limitless goodness, truth, and beauty. Yet when we limit our search to the imminent, we flatten out transcendence and fail to trace the signal back to its source. The connection is dropped and satisfaction with it.

Meaning, creativity, and satisfaction correspond with the three Greek transcendentals of truth, beauty, and goodness. Each transcendental points away from itself to God, the fountain of all truth, beauty, and goodness. The Holy Spirit is the person of the Trinity who initially opens the mind to true meaning, continually inspires creativity, and together with the Father and the Son satisfies us with the goodness of God. Therefore, the most meaningful, creative, satisfying life possible is one lived *here in Spirit*. And the Spirit accomplishes this not by transporting us away from this life, but by transforming us in it.

How does he do this practically? That's what we'll explore in this book. As we follow the Spirit through the sweep of Scripture, beginning to end, we will explore who he is. He's quite stunning when you stand back to take him in. And we'll consider what he does. He's not given nearly enough press. As we do, my aim is to help you recover a present-tense relationship with the Holy Spirit, making him the constant reality of your life.

If you glance at the table of contents, you'll notice the chapters follow a general arc from creation to new creation. This keeps the big picture of the Spirit's creation-perfecting work in view, while allowing me to color in the chapters with reflections on how he influences the stuff of everyday life—things like culture, work, prayer, community, waking up, evangelism, suffering, sin and temptation, and our longings for peace. Individual chapters are like beads on a string: they can stand alone but do much better when they hang together. At the end of the book you will find questions for reflection and discussion. If you are reading on your own, take some time to pause and consider them. If you have a small group, consider discussing them together, taking a couple chapters at a time, to deepen your learning in community.

As you read and reflect, I hope you are encouraged to live the most meaningful, creative, satisfying life possible—a life lived here in Spirit.

Culture with the Spirit

I STEPPED INTO THE cool mountain air, stretched my arms out wide, and began to walk. To my right and down the bank the water rushed, foaming as it coursed over the rocks, its roar soothing my soul. Step by step, I followed the tributary of the Eagle River around the base of the Gore Mountain Range. Hymns spilled from my lips. My eyes climbed the peaks. I imagined mountain-biking down the mountain—the thrill, the dirt, the sweat. For some reason, it wasn't enough to simply walk.

Now on a mountain, I look out across the valley stunned by the jagged white-capped peaks in the distance and expansive summer mounts in the foreground. I thought, "Come winter, I'll be snow-boarding on those babies, carving side to side in the fresh, silvery white power."

I love walking in beautiful settings, but my thoughts often wander to doing something *on* them. Back home, around Town Lake, I observe the wobbly paddle boarders, fishermen's lines stretching from their tin-can vessels, and the rowers. With each smooth stroke of the oars, I am transported onto the water with them, cutting through creation with purpose and ease. Watching them inspired me to take on sculling.

It's like I want to have dominion over these places—snowboard the peaks, row the lake, bike the mountain—but I can do none of that without culture.

CREATOR SPIRIT

Culture is what we make of the world. It's taking the physical world and molding it into something else. Someone had the bright idea of taking rocks and smelting them into iron. Then someone else imagined that metal as a bicycle, put two wheels on it, and we were off to the races.

In 1936 a young engineer who had figured out how to transport bananas from plantations into railroad cars without bruising them devised the very first chair lift. Using a chair affixed to the back of a truck, he experimented with skier pick up. The Nebraska summer made it difficult to simulate the slippery experience of being scooped up on skis in the snow, so the skier stood on oiled down straw. Six oils later, they couldn't come close. Then over a beer someone suggested wearing roller skates. Perfect. After twenty attempts, they finally found a speed quick enough to lift people without injuring them. Railroad engineers devised the wheels, pulleys, and towers necessary to move passengers up and down the mountain. By 1936 Jim Curran's chairlifts were installed at the very first American ski resort in Sun Valley, Idaho. Now chairlifts move thousands of people up mountains in a matter of minutes so they can ski or snowboard down.

In the beginning God made the raw materials for human culture. The Father spoke and the Spirit hovered over the face of the primordial waters, bringing everything into existence (Gen 1:1-2).

I wish I could have watched it happen, listened to the hum of the Spirit's work. The Hebrew word for "hovered" is often associated with birdlike imagery. Imagine a bird flapping its wings over the waters before it makes a dive to catch its prey, then increase the decibels *a lot*. The holy bird forms beauty out of the formless, brings light into darkness, and makes water into the world (2 Pet 3:5).

If you think about it, this description is actually compatible with String Theory, which suggests that everything is composed of microscopic vibrating strings. Who is the Spirit? The hand of God striking the notes of creation. But he isn't alone.

St. Irenaeus described God as creating with "two hands." The other hand is the Son, "but in these last days he has spoken to us by his Son, whom he appointed the heir of all things, *through whom also he created the world*" (Heb 1:2). The Father did not create the world alone, but through the work of the Spirit and the Son. Irenaeus devised the two hands metaphor to refute a philosophy called Gnosticism, which assigned greater value to spiritual things and lower value to physical, created things. The Gnostics believed angelic intermediaries were required for humanity to access the "Absolute Being." Ingratiating these angels through ascetic and hyper-spiritual acts could bring people closer to the divine. Paul refutes an early form of this teaching when he writes, "These have indeed an appearance of wisdom in promoting self-made religion and asceticism and severity to the body, but they are of no value" (Col 2:23).

To debunk the Gnostics, Irenaeus emphasized Jesus as a mediator of creation, who together with the Spirit made and reconciled humanity to the Father. He writes:

> It was not angels, therefore, who made us, nor who formed us, neither had angels power to make an image of God, nor

any one else, except the Word of the Lord . . . as if He did
not possess His own hands. For with Him were always present
the Word and Wisdom, the Son and the Spirit, by whom
and in whom, freely and spontaneously, He made all things.

Gnosticism creeps into the faith today when Christians belittle
secular culture (music, art, film, etc.) or privilege "ministry" over
other forms of work, as though God doesn't want to get his hands
dirty with such things. On the contrary, God's two-handed approach demonstrates his value of the created order and what we
do with it. By including all three persons of the Trinity in the
creation act, Irenaeus demonstrated God is fully invested in his
creation. Each person played their part in God's opus, the cosmos—
the Father spoke, the Son fashioned, and the Spirit energized.
Irenaeus underscored what Genesis reveals—the whole created order
is spiritual, the very work of the Spirit!

> Each person played their part in God's opus,
> the cosmos—the Father spoke, the Son fashioned,
> and the Spirit energized.

The Spirit also *sustains* creation through his renewing power:

> When you send forth your Spirit, they are created,
> and you renew the face of the ground. (Ps 104:30)

The Spirit is behind harvest and springtime, gravity and thermo-
dynamics, general relativity and quantum mechanics. He promotes
order and beauty in our world, and if the Spirit were to withdraw,
all things would collapse. The Spirit is the sustaining, renewing
presence of God behind the laws of the universe. Reflecting on
this ministry of the Holy Spirit, Old Testament scholar Chris
Wright concludes, "The universe itself owes its being to the Spirit

of God. The Holy Spirit is the one who has been constantly sustaining and renewing creation ever since, so that the sun rose this morning for another new day, and there was breakfast on your table." So the next time you enjoy a good breakfast, remember to thank the Holy Spirit for the food on your table. Maybe even consider what he did to get it there.

CREATING IN GOD'S IMAGE

How do we get from harvest to breakfast, from God's good creation to the good of snowboarding? What role does the Spirit play in our making of culture? Our key is the image of God. Genesis 1:26 unlocks our understanding of what it means to be made in God's image: "Let us make man in our image, after our likeness. And let them have dominion over the fish of the sea and over the birds of the heavens and over the livestock and over all the earth and over every creeping thing that creeps on the earth." What does this tell us about the image of God? A lot can be said, but I'll mention just two primary things.

First, to be made in God's image means to *rule like God*. Adam and Eve, and all their kids, were created to be kings and queens of creation, to exercise dominion over all the earth. This is sometimes referred to as the *cultural mandate*. This mandate puts the stewardship of creation in our hands. We see it in action when Adam and Eve work in the garden of Eden (presumably fashioning tools to tend it), when Adam categorizes the animals, and when Adam and Eve design clothing from fig leaves. Adam and Eve pioneered the first Gore-Tex! These cultural artifacts were the direct result of carrying out God's commission to rule and subdue the earth (Gen 1:28).

So what role does the Holy Spirit play in the creation mandate? You probably noticed the plural pronouns in Genesis 1:26, where God says, "let *us* make man in *our* image." God the Father appeals to the Son *and the Spirit* in fashioning humanity. Later we're told that God "breathed into his nostrils the breath of life," probably referring to the Spirit's animation of humanity (Gen 2:7). The Holy Spirit not only creates and sustains the world but also provokes us to make something of it. He is the perfecting force behind creation. St. Basil writes, "Bethink thee first, I pray thee, of the original cause of all things that are made, the Father; of the creative cause, the Son; of the perfecting cause, the Spirit."

> The Holy Spirit not only creates and sustains the world but also provokes us to make something of it.

The second thing the image of God tells us is that we are to *relate like God*. Like the Trinity, we are meant to relate as persons in relationship, which means we give and receive love, share in equal dignity, and submit to one another in reverence (1 Cor 11:3; Eph 5:21). Saint Augustine identified the Trinitarian relationship in terms of love: Lover (Father), Beloved (Son), and Love (Spirit). This self-loving, self-giving, overflowing relationship of love is the foundation for human love, which has profound implications for all our relationships, most of all our relationship with God himself. We'll come back to this later. For now it's worth highlighting the Spirit as the love of God, given to us as a gift: "God's love has been poured into our hearts through the Holy Spirit who has been given to us" (Rom 5:5). The Spirit is the very affection of God planted in our hearts, reminding us that we are wildly loved by the Father through the Son. To bear God's image, then, is to create and relate like him, living in cultural stewardship and loving relationship.

CULTURAL STEWARDSHIP

What's your chairlift? The Spirit wants to empower you to make something of the world. You have real purpose. If you don't know where to begin, start by considering your vocation. Whatever work you do, assuming it's ethical, the Spirit wants to work with you to bless the world through it. How do we do that? There are a lot of ways, but I'll focus on one. Our work should be *excellent*. Guiding the Colossians in vocation St. Paul wrote, "Whatever you do, work heartily, as for the Lord" (Col 3:23). The word *heartily* means work done well. In fact, the Greek words behind it can be translated "from the soul," suggesting that excellent work is a way to worship God.

When I was a window cleaner, I found it difficult to do excellent work. Washing windows seemed so meaningless. So what if people will be able to see through their windows better for a few days? Plus, washing windows in the Texas heat can be almost impossible. In the summers the water would often evaporate right off the window before I'd even begun to squeegee. But the place where I felt the real challenge to be excellent was wiping the ledges. I knew some window cleaners didn't do it, but I also knew it left a sludgy, unattractive residue. I concluded that wiping the ledge in hundred-plus degree heat mattered because it meant working well for God. I remember numerous times getting into my car to drive to the next account, only to drive back to the account I had already finished to wipe the ledges I overlooked. Although I missed a lot of ledges moving toward excellence, I came to understand that in the kingdom of God even window dressing counts. If you find your work uninspiring or mundane, take heart. It can be done as an act of worship if you do it well. Mow the best yard possible, run the numbers until you spot the anomaly, discipline the children even when it's hard. Do it because the Holy Spirit is with you, prompting you toward excellence.

Excellent work isn't just for God; it's for the world. When I drive over a bridge, I don't really care if the architects and construction workers were Christian or not. What I care about is whether or not they made a safe and sound bridge. A lot of bridges span the River Liffey in Dublin. One of the most famous is Ha'penny Bridge. The elliptical iron bridge spans over forty-two meters and stands out because of its three external arched ribs that support it. Their cruciform design offers exceptional resistance but also gives the bridge a measure of distinction. Picture the squiggly bracket on your keyboard, only turned horizontal with the midpoint facing up. Atop each point sits a lantern. Initially each pedestrian had to pay a "half penny" to cross the bridge. This divided social classes until the toll was removed and it was dubbed a bridge for all people. In its early years just a couple hundred people would cross the bridge each day. Today Ha'penny carries thirty thousand people safely across the Liffey each day.

Not all of us build bridges though. I once heard a professor, Miroslav Volf, give a lecture on the meaning of work. He told the story of being at a social function where he asked a man what he did for a living. The man responded, "I install urinals." What would you have said in response? Kind of a conversation stopper. Volf responded by thanking him for promoting good sanitation because without it our cities would quickly turn into cesspools. Whether you install pacemakers or urinals, your work matters to God and can serve humanity. Make the best thing you can.

Excellent work promotes human flourishing. Our work can contribute to human safety (construction), social justice (social and legal work), economic stability (business), and recreation (entertainment and the arts), to name a few. As the Ha'penny Bridge story shows, human care doesn't have to be at odds with a good aesthetic. Apple also strives for this. Commenting on his commitment to great design, Jony Ive, Apple's senior vice president of design, said: "I think that one of the things that just compels us is that we have a sense that, in some way, by caring [about design], we are actually serving humanity. People might think it's a stupid belief, but it's a goal—it's a contribution that we can hope we can make, in some small way, to culture." Ive sees excellent design as a contribution to culture. I'm grateful for his vision of culture making as I type away on my sleek MacBook Pro. The beautiful design not only serves me, but inspires me to write a well-crafted book that will serve you. In fact, we're compelled *by the Holy Spirit* to create culture that promotes human flourishing, which brings glory to God.

> We're compelled by the Holy Spirit to create culture that promotes human flourishing, which brings glory to God.

Now what do you do if you don't enjoy your work? A member of our church once shared they were starting to feel like they weren't called to their current job. He said, "Warren Buffet says he gets up every day and loves to go to work. Isn't that the way it's supposed to be?" I responded by suggesting that Buffet probably hasn't always felt that way about his work, jokingly reminding him he isn't Warren Buffet! Truth be told, the majority of people in the world work very "unfulfilling" jobs. Os Guinness, author of

The Call, reminds us, "To find work that perfectly fits our callings is not a right but a blessing." It's important to remember our primary calling is not to self-fulfillment but to serve Christ, to honor our Creator by working well, not by waiting for the dream job.

Our mandate to create fits into God's bigger mission for all creation. In the words of Colin Gunton, "Creation is a project. As created, it is perfect because it is God's project. . . . But it is not perfect in the sense of complete. It has somewhere to go." God has set the cosmos into motion, but with a grand mission—to redeem and perfect it over time (Col 1:20). The Holy Spirit is behind this creation-perfecting work, and we are integral to God's project. As his project developers, we are called to work with the Spirit to perfect all creation. But to do this well, we need to know the Spirit better.

More Than a Force

Iɴ ᴛʜᴇ Sᴛᴀʀ Wᴀʀs spinoff film *Rogue One*, Donnie Yen plays a blind warrior named Chirrut. Whenever Chirrut encounters a crisis he repeats the mantra, "I am one with the Force. The Force is with me. I am one with the Force. The Force is with me." Then "the Force" calms and empowers him to kick some Empire tail. My first couple decades as a Christian, I treated the Holy Spirit like a silent force in the Trinity. I loved Jesus, went to church regularly, discipled others, and even took mission trips around the world, but I assumed the Spirit's power. No mantras, no communication, no real recognition of the Spirit's presence. I believed the Spirit was essential for saving faith, gospel witness, personal change, and miraculous things, but I didn't *know* the Spirit. I had reduced him to a mystical force.

WHO IS THE SPIRIT?

If the Spirit isn't a mystical force, then who is he? In the film *Million Dollar Baby*, Clint Eastwood's character, Frankie, has a hard time with the Holy Spirit. After mass he exits the church building and tracks down the priest. The priest cynically asks, "What's confusing you this week, Frankie?"

Frankie replies, "Oh, it's the same old one-God, three-God thing."

The priest responds, "Most people figure out by kindergarten it's about faith."

Frankie retorts, "Is it sorta like snap, crackle, and pop all rolled up in one big box?" You can tell the priest is offended by Frankie's comparison between the Trinity and Rice Crispies cereal. But Frankie persists, "What about the Holy Ghost?"

The priest: "He's an expression of God's love."

Frankie: "Jesus?"

The priest: "The Son of God."

Frankie: "What does that make him, some kinda demigod?"

It can be hard to sort out how to know God when there are three persons to relate to. Is the Holy Spirit an expression of God's love, a spiritual force, or something else? How does he relate to the Father and the Son? Contrary to the priest's response, questions like these require more than "faith." On the very first page of his book on the Trinity, St. Augustine reminds us that faith must seek understanding, a dictum he mined from his translation of Isaiah 7:9. Does the Trinity require faith? Absolutely, but Christian faith works through reason, not against it. Sunday

> Christian faith works through reason, not against it.

school answers don't cut it when it comes to the Trinity. And of all the persons in the Trinity, the Holy Spirit seems like the hardest to know. Do you know the Holy Spirit? I mean really know *him*, not just his gifts or doctrine about him. Who is the Holy Spirit?

THE ACTIVITY OF THE SPIRIT

Let's return to Frankie's line of questioning, the whole one-God, three-God thing. Is the Holy Spirit fully divine? Well, the Bible doesn't just come right out and say, "The Holy Spirit is God," not because this isn't true but because the Bible isn't a theological textbook. However, St. Paul does say "Now the Lord is the Spirit," and he repeats this claim in the next verse (2 Cor 3:17-18). This is even more profound than calling the Holy Spirit God. The reason for this is that "Lord" is a reference to YHWH, the sacred name of God revealed to Israel, the "I AM." So, when Paul says the Lord is the Spirit he is including the Holy Spirit in the very identity of YHWH. He could make no higher claim regarding the divinity of the Spirit, yet the Bible is often more subtle in its doctrinal expression.

The Scriptures are composed of diverse genres of literature with coherent theological themes running through all of them. But it's not mere literature; it was written to specific people in specific places in specific times. It's a historical document. The Bible's specificity is part of its wonder. It is able to communicate eternal unchanging truths about God to frequently changing historical and cultural contexts. It is personal, engaged, and human and simultaneously universal, holy, and divine. For this reason, questions like, "Is the Holy Spirit God?" must be answered from within certain contexts and the overall narrative flow of the Bible. Another way to say this is that theological themes *unfold*.

One way to watch the doctrine of the Spirit unfold is to trace his *activity*. For example, when the Spirit creates, he does not create alone. As we saw, a full reading of the Bible shows the Spirit creating *with* the Father and the Son. This tells us something about the Spirit's unique relationship to the other two persons of God. As the Old Testament unfolds, we discover that the Spirit also *rescues* in participation with the Father and the Son. The avian activity of the Spirit in Genesis 1:2 reappears at the end of the Pentateuch (the first five books of the Bible) in Deuteronomy 32:10-11:

> He found him in a desert land,
>> and in the howling waste of the wilderness;
> he encircled him, he cared for him,
>> he kept him as the apple of his eye.
> Like an eagle that stirs up its nest,
>> that flutters over its young,
> spreading out its wings, catching them,
>> bearing them on its pinions.

Here we see the Lord hovering over the wilderness like a bird to create *a people*.

These images are very deliberate and are meant to show the Lord doing the same thing the Spirit does, but in this case to "create" a people by rescuing Israel. The narrative details point the reader toward a theological conclusion—*the Spirit and the Father are one and work together to accomplish their purposes.* In fact, all three persons of the Trinity work together to seek us out in the wilderness, encircle us with favor, and lift us out of our wickedness to enjoy apple-of-his-eye affection. The Spirit alerts our hearts to the rescuing, guiding love of God.

In the New Testament, the holy bird reappears at the baptism of Jesus, alighting on the Son as the Father speaks from heaven saying, "This is my beloved Son, with whom I am well pleased" (Mt 3:16-17). Have you ever thought about what the Spirit is doing here? Why he is present? He is pledging his power for Jesus' mission, a theme we will expand on in chapter eleven. He is also, together with the Father, celebrating his love of the Son. Before Jesus even lifts a finger to engage in public ministry, the Spirit and the Father remind Jesus of their mutual delight in him.

The Spirit is also present with you, crying out to remind you that you too are a son, a daughter, wildly loved before you do a single thing for God. This is a life-altering reality, that the all-satisfying love of God rushes toward us, apart from merit. It can also be incredibly difficult to comprehend and enjoy.

Sometimes when I correct my son, his head will drop and body curve in, as he darts away to bury his face in a corner. Wallowing in shame, it's hard for him to witness the love of the Savior. I'm trying to teach him that shame drives him to a corner, but conviction will drive him to Christ.

Acknowledging our sins to God can be hard because it requires admission of failure. It takes us down a notch. But even when we fail, God still loves us. We need not turn away in shame for not living up to our own standards, but can cast ourselves on the Father's love because Christ has kept his standard for us. God does not redeem us to leave us stranded in a never-ending battle with shame. He rescues us because he delights in us:

> He brought me out into a broad place;
> he rescued me, because he delighted in me. (Ps 18:19)

He rescues you, not merely as a trophy, but because *he delights in you*. Will you open yourself up to that love poured out into your heart in the Spirit? Sometimes I have to remind my son, "Son, no matter what you do, God is nuts about you." God is nuts about you too, and he sent his Spirit into your heart to remind you. The Spirit alerts us to the Father's undying love and prompts us to return to him over and over again (Gal 4:6).

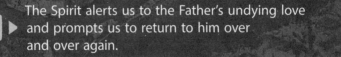

The Spirit alerts us to the Father's undying love and prompts us to return to him over and over again.

The Spirit's presence at Jesus' baptism also signals God's rescue mission has begun! As he hovered over Israel to create a people, he now hovers over the Son to create a people rescued by the love of God. So when sinners repent with faith in Jesus, they too are baptized, signifying God's rescuing love *and* his gospel commission. As Jesus was sent to proclaim the gospel, so too we are sent to spread the hope of God's undying love for the world in the death of Christ.

The rescue mission was hatched and secured with each person of the Godhead. The Trinity is at your back. So it comes as no surprise to find the Holy Spirit present at Jesus' baptism, where he is eternally imprinted on Jesus' commission to baptize in "the name of the Father, and of the Son, *and of the Holy Spirit*" (Mt 28:19). The Spirit is one with the Father and the Son, not only in the work of creation but also in redemption. As his creating and rescuing activity shows, the Spirit is indeed God (see also 2 Cor 13:14; 1 Pet 1:1-3; Jude 20-21; Mt 17:5).

THE ATTRIBUTES OF THE SPIRIT

As the doctrine of the Spirit unfolds, his deity is also expressed through *attributes* he shares with the Godhead. In the Old Testament God is often described as eternal:

> The eternal God is your dwelling place,
> and underneath are the everlasting arms. (Deut 33:27)

Similarly, the Holy Spirit is described as eternal: "How much more will the blood of Christ, *who through the eternal Spirit* offered himself without blemish to God, purify our conscience from dead works to serve the living God" (Heb 9:14). In fact, the three persons of the Trinity are the only truly eternal, uncreated things.

Consider the attribute of holiness. During his vision of Yahweh, Isaiah describes God as "holy, holy, holy" (Is 6:3). This threefold cry is used to emphasize the thorough and perfect holiness of God. "Holy" is affixed to the Spirit's very name (Ps 51:11; Is 62:11; Mk 1:8; Rom 15:13)! There are other attributes the Spirit shares with the Father and the Son. As you read over this list consider looking up some of these Scriptures. Pause to reflect on how these descriptions of the Spirit might change or intensify how you relate to the Spirit: eternal (Jn 14:16; Heb 9:14), omnipotent (Job 33:4; Ps 104:30), omnipresent (Ps 139:7-10), omniscient (Is 40:13; 1 Cor 2:10), holy (Ps 51:11; Lk 11:13).

ATTRIBUTES OF THE SPIRIT
Eternal (Jn 14:16; Heb 9:14)
Omnipotent (Job 33:4; Ps 104:30)
Omnipresent (Ps 139:7-10)
Omniscient (Is 40:13; 1 Cor 2:10)
Holy (Ps 51:11; Lk 11:13)

About sixty percent of self-identifying evangelicals claim the Holy Spirit is a force, not a person. They frequently refer to him as an "it." If they are correct, the Holy Spirit cannot be known, not like we know a person. But Scripture refers to the Holy Spirit *as a person*. To be clear, the Spirit is not a person in the sense of possessing a human body, but in the sense of possessing personal qualities. The Spirit speaks, teaches, guides, and intercedes. He can be obeyed, lied to, and grieved. Jesus refers to the Spirit using personal pronouns: "*He* will glorify me, for *he* will take what is mine and declare it to you" (Jn 16:14). Like the rest of the Trinity, the Spirit is relational because he is a divine person. These personal qualities, together with his divine activity and attributes, reveal the Spirit's rightful place among the Father and the Son. Consider how this list of personal qualities might influence the way you relate to the Holy Spirit. The Spirit speaks (Acts 13:2), teaches (Jn 14:26), guides (Acts 8:29), intercedes (Rom 8:26), is obeyed (Acts 10:19-21), is lied to (Acts 5:3), and is grieved (Eph 4:30).

> **THE SPIRIT'S PERSONAL QUALITIES**
> Speaks (Acts 13:2)
> Teaches (Jn 14:26)
> Guides (Acts 8:29)
> Intercedes (Rom 8:26)
> Is obeyed (Acts 10:19-21)
> Is lied to (Acts 5:3)
> Is grieved (Eph 4:30)

WORSHIPING THE SPIRIT

As a person, not a substance or mere force, the Spirit is someone to be known, relied on, enjoyed, and worshiped. The Spirit is fully divine and not inferior to the Father or Jesus. Returning to the debate we mentioned in chapter one, the first council of Nicaea (AD 325) only included a brief statement about the Holy Spirit, "And [we believe] in the Holy Spirit." But in AD 381 the Nicene Creed was revised to include a fuller statement regarding the Spirit. The description is stunning: "And [we believe] in the Holy Spirit, the Lord and Giver of life, proceeding forth from the Father, co-worshiped and co-glorified with Father and Son, the one who spoke through the prophets; in one, holy, catholic and apostolic church." In this expanded statement, the Spirit is recognized as Lord and worshiped alongside the Father and the Son. Why? Because the Holy Spirit is fully God deserving our adoration and praise. He is more than a force. As the official prayer of the Blessed Order of the Trinity states, "Glory be to the Father, and to the Son, and to the Holy Spirit. As it was in the beginning, is now and will be forever. Amen."

4

Renewing All Things

JAMES HALLIDAY'S CREATION utterly changed the world. It changed the way people spent time, formed relationships, and sought satisfaction. Money inside the OASIS eventually became more valuable than money outside. OASIS is a massive multiplayer online virtual reality game that engages all the senses through virtual-reality goggles and haptics, allowing the player to buy, sell, travel, build, befriend, attack, or meander inside a seemingly endless universe.

Commenting on this fictional universe, author Ernest Cline writes, "In the OASIS, you can become whomever and whatever you want to be. You could log in and instantly escape the drudgery of your day-to-day life. You could create an entirely new persona for yourself, with complete control over how you looked and sounded to others." This is an apt description of life *apart* from the Spirit.

When we live apart from the meaning, creativity, and satisfaction of the Spirit, we are bound to shape a persona we imagine will satisfy others. We begin to dress, think, behave, and speak in ways we hope will be acceptable or impressive to people we esteem. This creates a kind of death to reality. The Spirit, however, redeems our search for meaning and satisfaction, not by generating personas but by regenerating us into a new person. This puts us in touch with real life and peace. St. Paul writes, "For to set the mind on the flesh is death, but to set the mind on the Spirit is life and peace" (Rom 8:6).

PROMISE OF PERSONAL RENEWAL

In order to become a new person, we have to first admit our need for renewal. The need is evident everywhere. Headline after headline highlights our depravity: idolatry, war, deception, lust, pride, and envy. Scrolling through my news feed this morning, I saw headlines about the death of a legendary editor, the snobbery of President Trump, the resurgent fashion of displaying cleavage, and test missiles being fired "unrelated" to North Korea. I clicked on a story about Iceland idolizing Canadian Prime Minster Trudeau. Apparently Icelanders are so infatuated with Trudeau they created t-shirts that depict a Canadian landscape in reds and yellows, with a shirtless, ripped Trudeau smack dab in the center. Think Bruce Lee T-shirt but with Trudeau in his place. Bare-chested glory. It reminds me of the self-infatuated, viral image of Vladimir Putin riding bare-chested on a horse. That's the depravity "out there." But when we read the news, we hold it at arm's length, rarely including ourselves in the sins of the world.

Actually, our self-perception is about as accurate as a carnival mirror. Our moral distortion is a reflection of our spiritual distance from the goodness and beauty of God. The simple fact is we need new life because of our *incongruence* with God. We all possess a self-absorbed inwardness that puts us at odds with God's glorious holiness. Why are we like this?

A more liberal response would say our problem is negative influences. What we need is positive influences. But if you actually stop to think about it, this is quite an insult. This implies I am a prisoner of my circumstances, a product of my influences. My desires, dreams, hopes, and actions are futile.

On the other hand, a more conservative perspective sees the world as full of sinners, excepting the yours-truly conservative. It's the non-Christians that are bad; Christians are the good guys. But the Bible doesn't really talk like this. It's more sweeping and honest.

The Bible says we're all incongruent with God, not because of our influences, or even ultimately because of our sins, but because of our natural condition as enemies of God (Rom 1:18-32; 5:10). The condition is universal. No one has avoided infection. Apart from the renewing work of the Holy Spirit, we are all depraved, separated from the luminous glory of God.

How then does God deal with our spiritual and moral incongruity? Paul writes:

> For we ourselves were once foolish, disobedient, led astray, slaves to various passions and pleasures, passing our days in malice and envy, hated by others and hating one another. But when the goodness and loving kindness of God our Savior appeared, he saved us, not because of works done by us in righteousness, but according to his own mercy, by the washing of regeneration and renewal of the Holy Spirit. (Titus 3:3-5)

The irreconcilable difference between God and us is reconciled in a "but." A radical wave of mercy drenches us in the goodness and love of God, and we come out washed, forgiven, reconciled, and renewed. This is the result of Christ's work, not our works. But how can we get Christ's work to work for us? The Holy Spirit takes up the sin-absorbing sacrifice of Jesus on the cross and applies it to us so we can escape God's wrath and enjoy his favor forever. He washes us like new. The Holy Spirit is the wave and Christ the water. Together they work to make us a new creation.

But what exactly becomes new? Many things change when we are regenerated by the Holy Spirit. We receive new gifts (1 Cor 12), enter a new family (Eph 4), and possess an entirely different way of looking at the world (Rom 12). However, our essential personality is not altered. I am still Jonathan Dodson and you are still you. This is no invasion of the body snatchers, or a Doctor Who regeneration altering your entire physique. What is fundamentally renewed is our relationship with God. Now, instead of straddling our egos at a distance from God, we become infatuated with him. We desire to see his beauty, adore his glory, and enjoy his grace. In fact, *God comes to dwell in us* so we can know, worship, and enjoy all three persons of the Trinity. Paul writes, "Do you not know that you are God's temple and that God's Spirit dwells in you?" (1 Cor 3:16). The indwelling Spirit of God enables us to do all kinds of new things like resist temptation, obey God's commands, and delight in his presence. Speaking of the Holy Spirit Jesus says, "You know him, for he dwells with you and will be in you" (Jn 14:17).

The notion of a Spirit dwelling inside of us sounds weird and far out, but artists and philosophers have long acknowledged the need for a divine spirit. National Public Radio's Ann Powers describes the vocals of Alison Krauss as "a holy spirit wafting through the pop world." Musicians often insist their songs come from a kind of holy muse. Lucilius the Roman philosopher wrote, "A holy spirit indwells within us, one who marks our good and bad deeds and is our guardian." When people get in touch with the depth of human experience, or the height of artistic expression, they often reach for a holy spirit. They recognize their need, as well as a power, that transcends themselves. We've seen that the Spirit inspires creativity, but Jesus promises something even more: "In that day you will know that I am in my Father, and you in me, and I in you" (Jn 14:20). What's he saying? Jesus is saying when the Spirit indwells us, *he put us in Christ and Christ in us*, what's often called union with Christ.

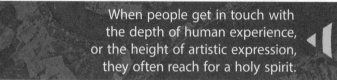

When people get in touch with the depth of human experience, or the height of artistic expression, they often reach for a holy spirit.

UNION WITH CHRIST

If the gospel were a dartboard, union with Christ would be the bullseye. It is the headline of the good news. The Spirit descends on us prompting faith in Jesus so we can be mystically and eternally united with him. How does this work? The Spirit enables us to enjoy Christ by making his work stick to us. As a result, when God looks at us he sees, not primarily our flawed nature or sinful behavior, but the flawless nature and behavior of Christ. To be united with Christ is to be covered up with his goodness.

One Halloween I bought a brown mullet wig, went to Goodwill and found a black John Cena t-shirt and cut the sleeves off. Then I put on some of the rattiest, tightest jeans I could find and shoved them into my old cowboy boots. Nobody recognized me at the neighborhood Halloween party. Unsure who I was, some neighbors edged away as I moved through the crowd. The costume was so good, they didn't have a clue who I was. But when they found out, they couldn't stop oohing and aahing over me, asking me questions about where I got the idea and the costume. They loved it!

When the Spirit places us in Christ, God the Father oohs and aahs over us. We're no longer defined by our sins and struggles. He's not put off or disinterested; he's drawn to us. Through the Spirit, Jesus' goodness becomes our goodness, his beauty our beauty. The difference between my redneck outfit and union with Christ is that God gives us true beauty. He knows our clothing in Christ isn't a costume. We become an actual new creation (2 Cor 5:17). The old, sinful, judgment-deserving person is exiled and a reconciled, acquitted, forgiven, renewed version of ourselves takes her place. The Father relates to us based on our new union with Christ, which frees us from fashioning personas. The indwelling Spirit gives us freedom to be our true selves in Jesus.

> Through the Spirit, Jesus' goodness becomes our goodness, his beauty our beauty.

At this point you may be thinking, *Okay, union with Christ by the Spirit sounds great, but you have no idea how hard my marriage is, or how demanding work can be, or the obstacles I face.* I don't, but Jesus does. And he says, "Peace I leave with you; my peace I give to you. Not as the world gives do I give to you" (Jn 14:27). Jesus' peace enters our hearts through the Spirit, but it can also leave our hearts through the world. What makes the difference?

Worldly peace is derived from secular tactics. One tactic is peace by *strategy*. Say a problem pops up at work. How do you respond? You develop a *strategy* to deal with it. The code you need to write, the information you need to gather, the words you must say. We strategize our problems. For example, when our children were young and one of our kids got sick, we'd google for info on it and scan some articles. After reading WebMD, we basically deduced our kid would never walk again. Our strategy made our stress go through the roof. More information doesn't bring peace. It can help us diagnose, but it's not a panacea for anxiety.

The problem with strategies is they don't secure peace. At best they solve superficial problems. Jesus says, "Not as the world gives do I give." His peace addresses the deeper problem of needing to trust the outcome of my child's health to him. How? United with Christ, we are free to be honest with our fears, but we're also invited to trust the outcome of his sovereign love. I am so relationally secure in Christ, I need not manufacture a false peace by mastering my child's future through research. Relying on strategy, we eject from the life and peace of the Spirit.

> United with Christ, we are free to be honest with our fears, but we're also invited to trust the outcome of his sovereign love.

Another strategy we employ is the peace of *escape*. When the going gets tough or the future looks bleak, we sometimes resort to escape. My go-to escape is the movies. If I've had a particularly heavy week in pastoral counseling, I'll duck into the theater for some relief. Don't get me wrong, good culture can bring good relief. But when I walk out of the movies the demands are still there. You can get a pedicure, binge Netflix, avoid people altogether, or just pine for the weekend, and peace still doesn't come.

Escape is momentary. Jesus' peace is lasting. Why? Because *it faces reality with ultimate rest*. I don't have to be crushed by other's struggles because Jesus is their rest, not me. You can endure a rough day and sleep well with deadlines at work because God doesn't sleep or slumber. Do excellent work and trust the results to Christ. The Spirit is there, prompting us all along the way, not to trust in escape but to trust in Christ. Escape is temporary. Union with Christ is forever.

But what if you're having a hard time finding peace? You don't have to fake it. We can bring the intensity of our frustration, the sourness of our disappointment, and despair of doubt to Christ and find sympathy. Jesus knows what it's like to be you. He doesn't expect you to be God; that's what he's for. Covered with his goodness and beauty we don't have to fake it. Real peace comes, not by hiding failures but by admitting them to Jesus. Be honest as you can about your own heart. Jesus died and rose to give us costly, precious peace. Don't try to improve on it. The Spirit is prompting us toward his peace, Jesus' very own peace—"*my* peace I give to you." How do we receive this peace? One way that's been really helpful for me is to begin each day praying over my responsibilities. I glance at my calendar in the morning before I start work, and I try to hand each meeting, each person, each scenario to the Lord by naming them aloud (including the results and how those make me look). If I miss some things, I try to pray through them as they pop up during the day. When I don't do this, I can tell. I'm more critical and easily irritated. But when I do it, the Spirit makes good on life and peace.

GOSPEL METAPHORS

Union with Christ is just one of the gospel metaphors the Spirit actualizes for us. We have already covered regeneration or new creation. Moving further out from the bullseye, we find redemption, justification, and adoption. None of these would be available to us apart from the Spirit. The Spirit is the one who applies these benefits and helps us believe them when we struggle to cherish them or conceive of them as true (Gal 3:5; Jude 20). The Spirit is the "voice" of our redemption. When we struggle to believe we are forgiven, or if there is a bright future ahead, the Spirit nudges us to trust in Jesus, to take up our Bibles and remember, to bank on his redeeming grace.

When Jesus redeems us, he makes it possible for us to receive the Spirit (Gal 3:13-14), who in turn cries out for the redemption of our bodies sealing us for the "day of redemption." As it turns out, the regenerating power of Doctor Who may not be that far off. The Spirit yearns for the day when our bodies will be glorified, possessing new properties like those of the risen Christ. This is the consummation of Christ's redemptive work (Rom 8:23; Eph 4:30). The Holy Spirit raised Jesus from the dead and raises us up with him to *justify* us, making us right with God (Rom 4:25). Finally, the Spirit is the "Spirit of adoption," bearing witness to our status as loved and accepted sons and daughters of God (Rom 8:14-17; Gal 4:4-7). The Holy Spirit is the agent who credits these marvelous gospel graces to us.

A RENEWED WORLD

The Spirit doesn't limit these graces to his people. He also promises a day when these truths will shape the whole universe. Each gospel metaphor is applied *cosmically*. This means that while we live in a very imperfect world, shot through with sin and sorrow, the future we want is on the way. Taking into account what we've learned about the Creator Spirit, it makes sense he would continue his perfection of creation *through the gospel*. Each gospel metaphor has a bigger application to the cosmos. Jesus describes a coming *regeneration of the whole world* (Mt 19:28)! Peter describes a new heavens and earth where everything is "put right" or *justified* so that righteousness and justice can move into the neighborhood permanently

(2 Pet 3:13). Paul tells us the *adoption* of the sons of God triggers the healing of all creation (Rom 8:18-25). And the whole world is *reconciled* to God by the blood of Jesus' cross (Col 1:20). Finally, all things will be *unified* or summed up "in Christ" so that Christ is all in all (1 Cor 15:28; Eph 1:9-10). The Spirit is integral to this cosmic work. He makes sure that goodness, truth, and beauty converge forever in Christ and his new creation.

When the creator of the OASIS died, he left behind a massive fortune but chose not to name an heir. Instead, he buried an Easter egg inside the game promising his entire fortune to whoever could find it in his virtual universe. In the closing chapter of the Bible, the Spirit beckons us toward the ultimate Easter egg, an eternal inheritance that far outstrips the promise of OASIS (Rev 22:17). Consider this cosmic inheritance:

> Then I saw a new heaven and a new earth, for the first heaven and the first earth had passed away, and the sea was no more. And I saw the holy city, new Jerusalem, coming down out of heaven from God, prepared as a bride adorned for her husband. And I heard a loud voice from the throne saying, "Behold, the dwelling place of God is with man. He will dwell with them, and they will be his people, and God himself will be with them as their God. He will wipe away every tear from their eyes, and death shall be no more, neither shall there be mourning, nor crying, nor pain anymore, for the former things have passed away." (Rev 21:1-4)

5

The Spirit of Silence

ALTHOUGH I COULD have passed a basic theology test on the Spirit, I would have flunked a relational test, if there ever was such a thing. I pretty much neglected the Spirit for two decades, but then, one chilly winter day in the quiet guestroom of our garage apartment, my relationship with him changed. It hit me. The Holy Spirit is a he, not an "it," a person to be known, listened to, and worshiped. I collapsed to my knees choking out my utter disregard for the Spirit. The Lord met me with a sweet forgiveness and spiritual sensation that attuned me to the Holy Spirit. I began to scour the Bible afresh to rediscover who the Spirit is and what he does. As I did, I started to realize that, while the Spirit had spoken to me quite a lot over the years, I had mistaken his voice as my own *reason*. Others make an opposite mistake, interpreting any impression they have to "the Spirit." How do we discern the Spirit's actual voice? There are various forms of discernment. Let's begin with the most important one—Scripture.

HEARING GOD'S SPEECH

If Scripture is God's speech to us, we can't hear the Spirit unless we have the Bible open. The Bible is not a loose collection of spiritual sayings, a theological textbook, or a moral compass, though it is spiritual, theological, and moral. It fundamentally claims to be God's exhaled self-revelation: "All Scripture is breathed out by God" (2 Tim 3:16). This means it's not a Choose Your Own Adventure book. I loved reading those books when I was a kid because I got to make the decision in how the book ended. I'd be deep sea diving in the ocean for treasure and then have to make a decision: "To dive deeper, turn to page thirty-one. To come to the surface and see what's going on, turn to page sixty-eight." I remember coming to the top of the ocean, only to have surfaced too quickly and died from the bends. The end.

The Bible doesn't work like this. It has a predetermined end and a fixed meaning. This meaning is conveyed through God's own breath. The word for "breath," both in Hebrew and Greek, is also used to refer to the Holy Spirit:

> By the word of the Lord the heavens were made
> and by the breath of his mouth all their host.
> (Ps 33:6; see also Gen 2:4; Heb 3:7)

The Spirit also breathes through the authors of Scripture to communicate with us: "For no prophecy was ever produced by the will of man, but men spoke from God as they were carried along by the Holy Spirit" (2 Pet 1:21). Picture Scripture as cargo carried on a boat across a river. The cargo of God's speech to us is delivered by humans, through their unique personalities, experiences, and education, but uniquely preserved as God's speech by the current of the Holy Spirit guiding the cargo to its fixed destination. This cargo contains the sparkling treasure of God's speech. To hear God's voice, then, we must be immersed in Scripture, dependent on the Spirit to understand what God has lavishly given us. If we don't heed Scripture, we may mistake our reason or emotion for the voice of the God. The Holy Spirit is given to us so we can understand God's language and comprehend the things he has given to us: "Now we have received not the spirit of the world, but the Spirit who is from God, that we might understand the things freely given us by God" (1 Cor 2:12). The Spirit is eager to guide us into God's will.

But hearing the Spirit's voice through Scripture can sometimes feel like trying to hear someone over a band at a concert. How do we make out his voice? To hear the Spirit, we have to quiet the noise. One form of noise is busyness. Henry David Thoreau once wrote: "We have lost the art of being still and doing nothing."

Can you remember the last time you did nothing? Really, stop and think about it. I have to talk myself into doing nothing sometimes, and when I am doing nothing, I have to remind myself that it's okay to do nothing. I even have to shoo away the guilt for not being productive so I can just sit and enjoy grace. Occasionally when I'm reading the Bible, items for my to-do list materialize. They distract me and try to push God's words around my mind. Suddenly getting a task done feels more urgent than meeting with God!

Danish philosopher and father of existentialism Søren Kierkegaard wrote volumes of thought-provoking philosophy that required gobs of doing nothing. Yet in reflection he described himself as a spectator in life, someone who learned about the views and theories of others while contributing nothing to the greater base of knowledge. He envied "great men" who pursued interests with great success, while struggling to find his own purpose. As a result, he felt a profound sense of inadequacy. Do you ever feel inadequate? I think of mothers in our church who feel the pressure to accomplish something—well-disciplined children, organic, gluten-free diets, well-kept homes with inviting interior design, a stand-out hobby, side job, or great career. If they don't accomplish these goals, they feel like they don't measure up. We often mistake purpose for accomplishment.

Kierkegaard eventually saw through all of this: "Let us never deceive youth by foolish talk about the matter of accomplishing. Let us never make them so busy in the service of the moment, that they forget *the patience of willing something eternal.*" He came to the point where he realized the futility of busyness in the service of temporal things and began to value the importance of slow, patient eternal things. This is particularly challenging in our age, where we believe just the opposite—that we need to accomplish a bunch of great things in order to be purposeful. In this milieu, how do we hear the voice of the Spirit? We may need to begin by renouncing accomplishment, to throw off the claim that a meaningful life is based purely on what we do and instead learn to rest in what God has done. We must patiently set aside productivity to slow down enough to value the things of God, to silence other voices so we can make out the sound of his voice. To live here in Spirit.

STILL, SMALL VOICE

Most of the time the Spirit speaks in a still, small voice. You may recall this phrase from an episode in the life of Elijah the prophet. Elijah had just gone toe to toe with the prophets of Baal. In a spectacular triumph over the false god, the Lord sent fire down from heaven as a display of his power and presence, and Elijah hacked the pagan priests to pieces. Israel's king Ahab had married a pagan Phoenician princess named Jezebel, whose father was king and priest to Baal worshipers. Hearing of Elijah's massacre of her priests, Jezebel vowed to take his life, so Elijah did what any of us would do—he ran.

Elijah eventually found a cave to rest in where "the word of the Lord came to him" and asked Elijah why he was there (1 Kings 19:9). Elijah responded with his resume of faithfulness amidst the faithlessness of his people, twice asserting, "I, even I only, am left" (1 Kings 19:10, 14). Who can blame him for feeling tired and alone? He had contended with an evil enemy, been rejected by his people, and was running for his life. The Lord responded to him by appearing three times—in a great wind, an earthquake, and a gentle whisper. Only in the whisper, also translated "a thin sound," did Elijah hear God's voice.

It's nice to know the Lord speaks in such normal ways, but why did he choose to speak this way? Perhaps it was because Elijah had become accustomed to flashy signs of God's power and needed to slow down to know God's presence? It's easy to get carried away in ministry seeking big things for God, good things—more conversions, deeper transformation, increased church attendance, multiplied churches—and fail to seek God himself. For years when I went to church planting conferences one of the first questions I was asked was, "How many are you running?" Rarely was I asked, "What are you hearing from God?" Maybe Elijah needed to know that God longs to speak *to* him, not merely through him.

Elijah also seemed to be looking for direction. What's next? When we're exhausted or looking for direction in life, it can be tempting to look for a big sign, a word from a friend, an unusual providence, or something spectacular. I have a friend who was debating whether to move from Texas to Minnesota, and then one day in the midst of praying, a huge truck drove by with one word on it: MINNESOTA. Most of the time God doesn't drive an eighteen-wheeler by to answer our prayers. He speaks through the simple silence of his Word.

The "word of the Lord" came to Elijah, not in a whirlwind or an earthquake, but in the stillness of day. Hearing that voice requires stillness, silence, and meditation on God's Word. Elijah could have easily read the bigger signs and moved on without hearing the hush of God's voice. But he stayed in the moment, listening for God.

Typical forms of piety can make it hard for us to hear the Spirit speak through the Word. Some people think of themselves as "prayer people," while others think of themselves as "Bible-study people." Often both of them miss the still, small voice of the Spirit. Do you know why? Because they fail to warm their souls at the fires of *meditation*. In meditation the Spirit strikes Scripture and prayer together to ignite affection for God and illuminate the soul. Tim Keller has said, "If Bible study married prayer they would have little meditations running around."

> In meditation the Spirit strikes Scripture and prayer together to ignite affection for God and illuminate the soul.

Our ultimate aim in communion with God should not be a comprehensive understanding of a passage, nor an emotional experience in prayer, but a fresh encounter with the Lord, which comes through getting a sense of the truth on the heart. When this happens, a passage opens up in communion with God. What truth did Elijah need to hear? That he was not alone, that not "I, even I only, am left," but that the Lord was with him, and so were seven thousand others who had not bowed the kneel to Baal (1 Kings 19:18). It's easy to think we are all alone when things get hard, that nobody understands what we're going through. But comparison suffering never got anyone through the dark night of the soul. We all need what Elijah needed, a fresh encounter with the small, still voice of God and an assurance that we are not alone.

ONLY THE SILENT HEAR

Once we're still how do we hear? Josef Pieper's plain observation is actually quite profound, "Only the one who is silent can hear." In order to listen to someone, we have to stop speaking.

It's easy for me to reduce prayer to a verbal wish list, filled with things for me and things for others—good things, biblical things—but if I'm the only one speaking, how will I ever learn to listen? One of the things I had to learn early in marriage was how to listen and not interrupt. I had a particularly hard time being quiet during an argument. Incapable of allowing my wife to finish her sentences, I would interject excuses and self-justifications. To improve our communication, we began using a pillow. The person with the pillow could talk, and the person without the pillow could not. So my wife would share how I was hurting her feelings, and when she was finished talking she would hand me the pillow, and it would be my turn to talk. Only when I was silent could I truly hear her concerns.

Listening well isn't natural for a lot of us, but consider what your relationships would be like if you were the only one who talked or if you kept interrupting! Like any good relationship, hearing from the Lord requires time and a listening ear. The author of Ecclesiastes exhorts us, "Guard your steps when you go to the house of God. To draw near to listen is better than to offer the sacrifice of fools, for they do not know that they are doing evil. Be not rash with your mouth, nor let your heart be hasty to utter a word before God, for God is in heaven and you are on earth. Therefore let your words be few" (Eccles 5:1-2). A slow mouth and an unhurried heart can put us in the presence of God.

So how should we practice silence? Well, it begins by recognizing there's more to silence than not talking. There's technological silence, literal silence, and spiritual silence. In my experience, a combination of all three works best. When I put devices in sleep mode, move into the quiet of my study or God's creation, and ask the Spirit to speak to me, I find I am more prone to hear. Walking or kneeling is particularly helpful for me. These postures mimic listening. They put me in a place where my body says, I'm ready for something eternal.

Although silence is a marvelous means for reflection and rest, it isn't the ultimate end. Silence is for hearing God's voice. And if God's speech is found in Scripture, the Word is critical to discerning the timbre of his voice. When I get alone to hear from God, I've discovered three basic things that help me listen. First, instead of barreling into my chosen passage of Scripture, I pause and ask the Holy Spirit for *insight into God's Word.* When I don't do this, I tend to rely on my own education and reason, bypassing the Holy Spirit. Instead of assuming I can obtain the insight I need, this prayer puts me in a position for the Helper to help me. Remember, the Spirit has been given to search out all things, even the depths of God, and to reveal things to us (1 Cor 2:10). I often say this back to the Spirit asking him to guide me into communion with God, putting Bible reading in a relational, not purely rational, context. I once heard a preacher say, "The first thing I do in the morning is say, 'Help me Lord.'" That's not a bad way to start reading the Bible if you want to hear God's voice.

SPIRIT-LED BIBLE MEDITATION ◀
Ask the Spirit to:
Give me insight
Reveal my need
Create a response

Second, ask the Spirit *to reveal your need*. As our relentless search for accomplishment shows, we're poor authorities on what we need. The Spirit knows exactly what we need. Here's where the Spirit's omniscience really helps us, "Search me, O God, and know my heart! Try me and know my thoughts!" (Ps 139:23; cf. Ps 7:9; 17:3). You may need an encouragement, something to rejoice in. Or you may need a sin exposed to lead you to Christ, or perhaps a comforting word. Only the Spirit truly knows. Ask him to reveal your need.

Third, ask the Spirit *to create a response* to him. I am so tempted to leap over this. I tend to think if I can get the right insight, then I'll be able to do whatever God is asking. But apart from Spirit-created desire, I won't want to or may have a hard time responding the way he wants me to. John Frame describes several possible responses to Scripture: "God speaks so we can understand him and respond appropriately. Appropriate responses are of many kinds: belief, obedience, affection, repentance, laughter, pain, sadness, and so on." Ask the Holy Spirit to guide you in response to his Word. He may want you to shout aloud in praise:

> Praise the LORD!
> Praise the name of the LORD,
>   give praise, O servants of the LORD,

who stand in the house of the LORD,
in the courts of the house of our God! (Ps 135:1-2)

He may want you to act immediately in obedience to reconcile a strained relationship: "So if you are offering your gift at the altar and there remember that your brother has something against you, leave your gift there before the altar and go. First be reconciled to your brother, and then come and offer your gift" (Mt 5:23-24). He may want you to bask in his love, cry out in pain, or marvel at one of his attributes. Just ask the Spirit to guide you. He's eager to do it.

Perhaps this chorus we often sing summarizes what I've been trying to say:

We are listening to your word
Morning and evening we come
To delight in the words of our God
Give us eyes to see
Give us faith to hear
. . . that the Word has come
. . . that the Word is here.

That chilly day in the guestroom I realized that, although I believed the Spirit spoke, *I had not learned to listen!* I began listening and talking to the Spirit every day. It didn't take long for me to realize that you don't move from complete stranger to intimate friend overnight. It has taken time to undo old habits, but the Spirit has been with me every step of the way as I cultivate the patience of willing something eternal. That same patience is available to you—to live here in Spirit.

6

More Than Conviviality

In THE FILM *Notting Hill* there's an iconic dinner party scene where family and friends get together. After years of divorce and heartache, Hugh Grant's character has found an American woman, Anna, and is finally ready to introduce her to the family. Table discussion is marked by laughter, candid confession, and fighting for the last brownie. Conversation moves effortlessly from topic to topic. Everyone wants to be there. Each person is valued. Joy hangs over the table like a canopy. This is conviviality.

Conviviality is a word that comes from a Latin root meaning "banquet," suggesting a mood of full-bellied joy. It is something we all long for but, truth be told, we rarely experience. Why is that? Well, consider who's at the table—a young, wheelchair-bound wife facing reproductive challenges, a single man who struggles with loneliness and career advancement, and a socially awkward sister who declares upon meeting Anna that they will be best friends. Then there's Anna who confesses, "One day not long from now my looks will go and they will discover I can't act and I will become some sad middle-aged woman who looks a bit like someone who was famous for a while." Only when the real struggles come out do we begin to get a look at real community.

Community doesn't equal conviviality. Do you know why? Life is not a dinner party and people are not the feast.

People cannot consistently fill our bellies with joy. Life moves beyond the dining room into the living room, the bedroom, the garage, and out into the real world where we experience loss, conflict, pain, anger, loneliness, frustration, and disappointment. As long as we hang on to the expectation of conviviality in the place of community, we will be continually disappointed. Not that we won't experience full-bellied joy from time to time, but a proper vision of community refuses to demand conviviality as the norm. Instead, the Spirit gets us out of the dining room into the whole house, sharing the full gamut of life with others, the good times and the bad.

The Spirit shows us what it's like to live faithfully *here*—not just in the world to come. This begins with a Pentecost.

A UNIQUE PENTECOST

In chapter three, we saw that Old Testament prophets spoke of a time when the Spirit of God would be poured out "on all flesh." In Acts 2, this promise was fulfilled in Jerusalem at Pentecost. However, the Pentecost in Acts was not the first; there were actually many Pentecosts. In Greek the word means "fiftieth," referring to a Jewish festival that occurred fifty days after the Passover, when Israel was delivered from Egypt. Pentecost had been observed every year since the Passover, with the exception of when Israel was in exile. But when we get to Acts, Pentecost is different. Look at what St. Luke records:

When the day of Pentecost arrived, they were all together in one place. And suddenly there came from heaven a sound like a mighty rushing wind, and it filled the entire house where they were sitting. And divided tongues as of fire appeared to them and rested on each one of them. And they were all filled with the Holy Spirit and began to speak in other tongues as the Spirit gave them utterance. (Acts 2:1-4)

Does this description sound familiar? Can you recall other places in Scripture where we see a rushing wind and the presence of fire? In creation, the Spirit blows like a wind over the waters of the deep. After the Fall, a wind reappears when Adam and Eve turn their backs on God. We're told God comes searching for Adam "in the cool of the day," a phrase that can also be rendered "in the wind of the storm." After God delivered David from King Saul, David wrote a song describing the Lord as a rider on the wind:

> He rode on a cherub and flew;
>> he was seen on the wings of the wind. (2 Sam 22:11;
> see also Ps 18:10)

It is possible this is no idle breeze but the potent presence of the Spirit, from whom Adam and Eve try to hide. At the Exodus, a great east wind parted the Red Sea to deliver Israel from Egypt, and God led them through the wilderness by a pillar of cloud by day and a pillar of fire by night (Ex 13:21). During Israel's ultimate return from exile, God will accompany them "like a rushing stream, which the *wind* of the Lord drives" (Is 59:19). These wind and fire scenes are vivid images of the Spirit. So when we hear the rushing wind and see the fire blaze in the upper room at Pentecost, we are meant to anticipate yet another work of the Spirit.

What will the Spirit do? What sets this Pentecost apart? Did you notice wind and fire don't just hover over the inhabitants of the room—they inhabit them! The prophecy is fulfilled as rushing wind fills not only the house but all who are present, about a hundred and twenty people (Acts 1:15). The number is symbolic: the twelve tribes of Israel are symbolically multiplied and perfected through the number ten. The Spirit is creating a new Israel around the risen Christ. The twelve tribes of Israel will expand exponentially by incorporating people from every ethnic group to constitute the true people of God. How will this be accomplished?

The Spirit sends the one hundred and twenty out to testify to the person and work of the risen Christ. Immediately the disciples begin to share the gospel in languages they have never spoken! At this Pentecost the Spirit is sent into a fledgling church, in wind and in fire, to launch a new chapter in the mission of God.

RECONFIGURING COMMUNITY

What will the Spirit accomplish by indwelling his people? He enters us not just to apply the benefits of Christ, but also to get us on track with God's vision for the world. After the initial fall from grace, humanity failed to live up to God's image and original vision. We've gone about relating and creating not in his likeness but however we like. As a result, we muck up the creation project. So to get everything back on track, the Spirit conceives in us a new community and calls us into his mission. After the Jerusalem church's initial burst of evangelism and preaching, they normalize as a missionary community:

> And they devoted themselves to the apostles' teaching and
> the fellowship, to the breaking of bread and the prayers. And

awe came upon every soul, and many wonders and signs
were being done through the apostles. And all who believed
were together and had all things in common. And they were
selling their possessions and belongings and distributing the
proceeds to all, as any had need. And day by day, attending
the temple together and breaking bread in their homes, they
received their food with glad and generous hearts, praising
God and having favor with all the people. And the Lord
added to their number day by day those who were being
saved. (Acts 2:42-47)

This passage describes the primary elements of community:
apostolic teaching (gospel), devotion to one another (community),
and adding to their number daily (mission). Right off the bat the
first Christians devote themselves to gospel teaching, a message
focused on the life, death, resurrection, ascension, and promised
return of Jesus (Gal 1; 2 Cor 5:11-21). They gathered frequently
to hear the Scriptures taught, but their devotion wasn't in isolation.
It wasn't as if they restricted their attentiveness to the gospel to
individual quiet times only. They learned *together*, taking time
to enjoy one another's fellowship, sharing in the Lord's Table,
eating and drinking with gladness.

Since my wife is a realtor, I get to visit new homes with her
every once in a while. I have noticed a trend with some newer
homes—they're built without a dining room. Instead there's a short
bar in the kitchen and large media rooms. I can't help but notice
how this reflects a shift in our society's values. Less time delighting
in one another around the dining room table and more time wor-
shiping around the media room screen. We're not far away from
Ray Bradbury's dystopian living area, where video screens take up

an entire wall. These screens invade not only our homes but our relationships. Arcade Fire sings:

> Now, the signals we send are deflected again
> We're still connected, but are we even friends?
> We fell in love when I was nineteen
> And I was staring at a screen.

Despite all its benefits, social media can disrupt deep connection. Up to date on one another's lives, we can feel as though there's not much to talk about when we connect face to face. But this is thin community, where we mistake information for understanding. In-person conversation gives us an opportunity to understand how our friends are dealing with their experiences. We can ask how they are handling their anxiety or facing their fears, or what is so thrilling about their latest discovery. In the flesh, we can offer a hug, a supporting prayer, or a look of empathy. When we get face to face, community can thicken.

Fortunately, I have a reference point for the kind of community Luke describes. It brings to mind the kind of meals my wife creates around our kitchen table. The table is set, food spread out, dessert waiting in the stainless-steel fridge, but what we're all really there for is the fellowship. As soon as I've thanked the Lord for what we have, my wife begins to ask thoughtful questions. She gives people a place at the table. Often they get so comfortable they laugh like there's no tomorrow or cry to mourn an old wound. I feel the subtle presence of the Holy Spirit, prompting us at different times to console, confess, counsel, and encourage, all over food. This is our version of Spirit-formed conviviality.

When we first started our church, my wife would make home-cooked meals for the dozen or so people who would come over to our house on Wednesday nights. We learned one another's stories, chatted, laughed, dreamed, and prayed. As a family, we tried to invite people into our lives, not just to our meetings. We often sent out invites to everyone when we went out to eat or to the park with our kids. Sometimes people would join us, but most times they didn't.

I remember sending out an invitation to meet us at Chick-fil-A for dinner and one person showed up. Acts 2 felt like a pipedream. But God was teaching me something, the *patience* of willing something eternal. Spirit-filled community isn't instant; it's formed over time, against the challenges of an individualistic, data-consuming society. It requires taking the long view.

> Spirit-filled community isn't instant;
> it's formed over time,
> against the challenges of an individualistic,
> data-consuming society.

Eventually home-cooked meals by my wife were replaced with potluck meals by everyone. We began to connect with one another at different times and places, and it felt like community was getting thicker. Then Acts 5 happened.

In Acts 5 the couple Ananias and Sapphira deceive the community by misrepresenting profit from their sale of a piece of property. Acting like they were giving it all to help the community, they held back profit, giving a false impression of their generosity. The issue was not how much they gave, but that they lied *to the Holy Spirit*: "Ananias, why has Satan filled your heart to lie to the Holy Spirit and to keep back for yourself part of the proceeds of the land?" (Acts 5:3). Ananias was struck dead, and his wife soon followed, committing the very same sin.

Lies threaten community, but the truth builds it up. This is why Paul tells the Colossians to "let the word of Christ dwell in you richly" (Col 3:16). The "you" is plural, and the truth ferments in community through teaching and admonishment. This means that refusing to speak the truth of God's Word or avoiding gentle correction actually harms community. Here Peter refuses to cave into fear of what others might think. Can you imagine the gossip when he called a couple out for lying about their finances? How intrusive! Yet he faces down the cost so that the word of Christ can enrich the community. As a result, a reverent fear spread over the whole community, even among those outside (Acts 5:11). When a community feasts on the Word together, they end up filled with gratitude and praise that attracts attention (Col 3:16).

> When a community feasts on the Word together, they end up filled with gratitude and praise that attracts attention.

Since we are saved into a community, sin is never an individual affair. Sin is communal. Ananias colluded with Sapphira and their sin affected the community. The church lost a brother and a sister on the spot. But this was also an occasion to forgive as they had been forgiven. When we read Acts 2 in isolation from Acts 5, we will grow impatient and judgmental of our own community. But when we read them in concert, we will adjust our expectations of others, allowing for some dystopia in our utopian visions of church. For many this will require a reimagining of what church is supposed to be. When community gets hard, we are tempted to fantasize about other churches, compare strengths and weaknesses, judge and not forgive. Aldous Harding's lyrics capture the difficulty of reimagining this kind of love:

It can be so hard to forgive
It's not what I thought, and it's not what I pictured
When I was imagining, when I was imagining my man.

When imagining church, very often we leave out real love, the occasions for forgiveness.

Fortunately, God is not caught off guard by all this. As holy judge, he has the right to strike us all dead on the spot, but in Christ he mercifully refrains and forgives. He of all people knows how hard it is to forgive. Yet he chooses to work through crisis to create deeper community.

As sorrow entered our community, it broke across the private invisible lines we had drawn around ourselves. But God used crisis to knit us together—a father of two lost his livelihood, a spouse transgressed marital love, a worship leader got intoxicated, and a member abandoned the community in a hail of slurs and slander. Crisis and confession, repentance and faith, suffering and heartache put us in touch with one another. It created context for deeper community. It helps us look up from our screens and across the table. As Over the Rhine sings, "Pain is our mother; she makes us recognize each other."

But crisis also put us in touch with the one who holds us together—Christ our Redeemer. As people braved transparency and collapsed in confession, we learned how to support one another and forgive. On the evening a trembling leader confessed his hidden sin to the community, he was met with an outpouring of forgiveness, prayer, encouragement, tears, and help. I'll never forget what one woman said to me afterward: "I have never experienced *church* like this before. Thank you."

There were some exceptions to her response. We had to navigate disappointment, combat gossip, and learn to walk humbly together behind Jesus, but the Spirit was building his church and forming true community.

7

The Great Companion

SCANNING THE VALLEY BELOW, he searches for signs of life. Soft ash swirls over the blacktop. He knows their best bet is to stay close to the road. Father and son make their way along the perilous stretch, dodging in and out of abandoned houses and towns, scavenging for food. He keeps a pistol and a knife for protection. All they have is each other. The "truck people" patrol the road, preying on anyone and anything for food and water. A truck rolls by the edge of the forest where they are sleeping. The father wakes up, noticing the truck people fanning out through the woods. One of them grabs the boy and puts a knife to his throat, threatening to kill him. For a few tense moments, the father is threatened with separation from his son. The father quickly fires a shot right through the truck person's head. Shivering with fright the boy is scooped up by his father. They move on quickly, knowing the shot will only attract more people. Coming upon a lake, the father stops to wash the dried blood from his son's head. He thinks to himself: "All of this [is] like some ancient anointing. So be it. Evoke the forms.

Where you've nothing else, construct ceremonies out of the air and breathe upon them."

THE SEARCH FOR COMPANIONSHIP

Like many other authors, Cormac McCarthy uses the imagery of a road to explore the meaning of life. One of the central possibilities for meaning is companionship. Despite the bleakness of their post-nuclear world, the father-son relationship pulses with hope. Perhaps by depending on one another they will survive. As they snatch moments of intimacy, we detect the promise of meaning in a father's love for his son. Yet along the road they both daydream of more, not merely of more safety or sustenance, but of more companionship. The father's heart soars and withers under the memory of his wife. The son pines for friendship with other children. We are not meant to walk the road alone.

In the beginning God walked with his children in the Garden of Eden. After creating Adam, God saw it was not good for man to be alone, so he fashioned a companion. Interestingly, God did not excuse himself from walking with them after forging this perfect union. He knew Eve did not complete Adam, and Adam could not complete Eve. Humanity was made in *his* image, not in the image of the perfect couple but in the likeness of a holy Trinity. So God continued to walk with Adam and Eve in the cool of the day—until they walked out on him. Refusing to trust God, Adam and Eve ruptured fellowship with him for all humanity. We have been reeling ever since, looking for faithful companionship everywhere, except the one place it can be found, with the Father, Son, and Holy Spirit.

Christians often emphasize the importance of having a relationship with Jesus, and despite imperfect relationships with our own fathers, we intuitively recognize the value of relating to a heavenly Father. But companionship with the Holy Spirit is something vastly overlooked and unexplored. Richard Lovelace captures this problem well:

> This failure to recognize the Holy Spirit as personally present in our lives is widespread in the churches today.... Even where Christians know about the Holy Spirit doctrinally, they have not necessarily made a deliberate point of getting to know him personally. They may have occasional experiences of his reality on a hit-and-run basis, but the fact that the pronoun "it" is so frequently used to refer to him is not accidental. It reflects the fact that he is perceived impersonally as an expression of God's power and not experienced continually as a personal Guide and Counselor.

Sadly, what was true in 1979, when Lovelace wrote these words, is largely true today as well. Why is this the case? Conceiving of a relationship with a "spirit" is certainly more difficult than with a father or a son. However, the Spirit's relational names such as Helper and Comforter, together with his personal actions, transcend this conceptual difficulty. Perhaps what has hindered relationship with the Holy Spirit most over the past hundred years is an unhealthy preoccupation with his miraculous gifts. Like focusing on just a few character traits of a friend or spouse, narrowing our focus to a handful of the Spirit's gifts is bound to distort and obscure the relationship.

When I was young, I was attracted to my wife's gregarious, fun-loving personality. However, as I have known her over years I have come to appreciate the complexity and beauty of her whole person, including her wisdom, generosity, self-sacrifice, creativity, and resolve. Similarly, restricting our focus to debates about the Spirit's gifts of prophecy and tongues limits our appreciation and enjoyment of him.

Frozen in youthful perception, our narrowed perspective inhibits a maturing relationship with the Holy Spirit. Walter Klink notes, "The Spirit must stop being merely a debate over prayer languages and powerful healing and must become the constant reality of the Christian life and experience." In addition, attempts to conceive of the Holy Spirit as the "Infinite Spirit" of the universe or as merely an expression of the universal human spirit have not helped us relate to him as a definite person. Yet, as we have seen, there is ample biblical revelation regarding the personal nature of the Holy Spirit.

HELPING US THROUGH HATE

Have you ever felt alone, isolated, without someone to get your back? I've had stretches where I thought no one understood what I was going through. Hard times hit, family moves, friends desert you, and the feeling of abandonment sets in. What do you want more than anything in those moments? A friend who never leaves. A companion who will stick with you through thick and thin. Someone who will walk with you *through anything.* The Holy Spirit is that kind of person. In fact, Jesus said it was better for him to go away so that he could send the *Helper* to us (Jn 16:7).

"Helper" is easier to relate to than "Spirit." It puts a face on the Holy Ghost. But what exactly did Jesus mean by "Helper"? The Greek word *parakletos* can be translated various ways—helper, comforter, advocate—but is essentially "one who is called to someone's aid." The Spirit is someone who gets your back. Jesus explains, "But when the Helper comes, whom I will send to you from the Father, the Spirit of truth, who proceeds from the Father, he will bear witness about me" (Jn 15:26).

One way the Helper helps is by bearing witness to Jesus. When we're down, or feel like the world is against us, the Helper knows just what to do. He doesn't fluff our ego by telling us we're awesome and everyone else is dumb. He doesn't offer false hope by whispering sweet nothings in our ear. He tells us the truth because he is the "Spirit of truth." In moments of temptation and seasons of despair, he whispers the promises of God and words of comfort. He reminds us what is true.

Jesus' description of the Spirit as Helper occurs right after telling his disciples they will be hated by the world (Jn 15:18-25). Hate is a strong word. Whenever I hear one of my kids say, "I hate you," I quickly respond, "We don't use that word. Can you think of a different word?" Should Jesus be using a different word? Are we really *hated* by the world?

Over a million Christians were killed for their faith in the decade between 2000 and 2010. That's one hundred thousand martyrs a year. I'd say they qualify for being hated by the world. We know the Helper is certainly there for them, helping them hold fast to Christ when lined up in orange jumpsuits on a sandy beach and killed execution style. But what about the rest of us?

Up to this point, the disciples' experience of hatred hadn't really been physical. Not a drop of blood had been shed. They had been snubbed by friends and family, some put out of the synagogue, others mocked and sharply debated by the religious establishment. They experienced a kind of social hatred, marginalizing them within their own culture. For them being hated by the world was mainstream society saying, "You're not welcome here. Your views aren't valid. We reject your Messiah." So when Jesus says the world hates you, he's primarily referring to the world *system*, its way of seeing and shaping things, a viewpoint that privileges other ideologies and values over the gospel. This world-system hate is sometimes in your face, but often it's a understated snub.

I was meeting a friend with secular commitments for lunch when she asked me if I was writing another book. I eagerly told her I was, and she thoughtfully inquired what it was about. I said, "I don't have my elevator pitch down yet, but its essential message is that instead of finding our identity in a disembodied state of what others think of us, online or at work or whatever (being there in spirit), our true identity is found here in the present through faith in Jesus (being here in Spirit). It's about how walking with the Spirit of God affects everything from the culture we make to the God we worship."

She responded, "Yeah, we need to hear that message about being more present in the moment." Using her own worldview to redefine and reinterpret my explanation, she coopted my thesis and lopped off half of the book! She excised what she hated—the exclusive claim of Jesus as the best identity-giver through his Spirit—with a warm smile and a well-intentioned kindness, but it was an expression of the world's hate.

Perhaps you've had a similar experience or heard something like this in a conversation: "You don't believe *that,* do you?" "Do you take the Bible *literally?*" How does the Helper assist us in these kinds of situations? With Jesus gone, we need help from outside the system. We need an independent witness to *the truth* who can see things the way they really are. The Spirit bears witness, or testifies, to that reality. In the moment of hatred, the Spirit gives us faith to stand. One way to respond to these jabs is to ask a simple question: "Why do you believe differently?" "What do you mean by *literally?*" This allows us to winsomely absorb the blow while moving the conversation toward the truth. When my friend changed the meaning of my words, I did not back off my thesis. Instead, the Holy Spirit prompted me to continue talking with her and to pray for her. After we left, the Spirit also prompted a friend who was with me to comment on her reaction. It was nice to know I wasn't the only one who witnessed the minor offense.

Sometimes standing up for the truth is more painful. Several women in our church come to mind, women who have lovingly called their friends to repentance over gossip, sexual sin, and divisiveness, only to lose the friendship altogether. One woman in particular sought reconciliation with a friend after they had parted ways for over a year. She heard her friend's father died in a tragic car accident, so she reached out to express empathy and ask if she could attend the funeral. She was abruptly shut down and not permitted to attend. The loss of friendship was almost unbearable.

In the season of isolation, in the temptation to weaken in faith, the Spirit announces in the chamber of our souls, "Jesus is worth it. Jesus is better. Jesus is supreme." His acceptance is more enduring than that of friends, his love purer than a spouse's, and his gospel truer than ideologies peddled by this world.

> In the temptation to weaken in faith, the Spirit announces in the chamber of our souls, "Jesus is worth it. Jesus is better. Jesus is supreme."

If the Spirit doesn't stand up in my heart for that truth, for the superiority, beauty, and utter uniqueness of Jesus, I'll cave into the hatred. I won't stand up and love the world by insisting that Jesus is the way, the truth, and the life. I'll let their response roll over me unchecked, and I'll slowly believe bits of their worldview. We'll begin to think avoiding gospel conversations is a sure path to true acceptance, or sleeping with a non-Christian boyfriend is better than resting in what Jesus offers, or that more convenience and ease is what brings real happiness.

When we are walking in the Spirit, we will hear his silent witness to Jesus in our hearts, and in turn we will witness to others. When we receive the help of the Spirit, we are emboldened to help others. You see, the Spirit is more than a helping hand or an infinite force. He's the one who always gets our back. He is the companion who always tells the truth, the friend who never fails.

THE WALKING GOD

After Adam and Eve were sent out of the Garden, God only walked with humans again in a few cases before the arrival of Jesus. Enoch walked with God and then he "was not" (Gen 5:24). Both Noah and Abraham walked with God (Gen 6:9; 17:1), and God spoke with Moses as a man speaks to a friend (Ex 33:11). But after exile from Eden, most of God's people did not enjoy intimate companionship with him. The Lord did intervene to rescue Israel from their exile in Egypt, promising to walk among them in a more general way, if they kept covenant with him. Unfortunately, Israel rebelled against God, and God turned his face against them sending them into exile (Lev 26). Centuries passed without God walking among them.

But then Jesus arrived, walking quite literally with men, women, and children. His presence signaled the hope of God's renewed commitment to walk with his people. Can you imagine meandering the fields with Jesus, his hands brushing across the wheat stalks, while speaking intently with you? Very few had this opportunity.

And in just a few years Jesus was gone. Ripped away by death, his disciples mourned the loss of their Master and friend. They must have wondered, "Will God ever walk with us again? When will he return?"

The answer came rushing like the gusts of Eden. Blowing through the enclosed upper room where the disciples waited, the Holy Spirit filled the nascent church, fulfilling the promise, "And I will walk among you and will be your God, and you shall be my people" (Lev 26:12; 2 Cor 6:16). God was here, in Spirit, to walk with his people to the very end. Even as the church experienced persecution, it was marked by peace because they walked "in the fear of the Lord and in the comfort of the Holy Spirit" (Acts 9:31). The Spirit walked with each person who put faith in Jesus. In fact, walking in the Spirit became a kind of shorthand for life lived with God. Walking with him is to be in relationship with all three persons of the Trinity, but it seems the Spirit is the one who always trails behind. Some have insisted this is exactly how things are supposed to be.

J. I. Packer describes the Spirit as a floodlight meant to cast attention onto the building of Christ, while the floodlight itself goes unnoticed. He writes, "You are not in fact supposed to see where the light is coming from; what you are meant to see is just the building on which the floodlights are trained. . . . This perfectly illustrates the Spirit's new covenant role." While one of the Spirit's central roles is to draw our attention to Christ, his "floodlight ministry" is not to the exclusion of knowing him. Yet Packer goes on to say, "The Spirit's message is never, 'Look at me; listen to me; come to me; get to know me.'" To be sure, the Spirit is not narcissistic, but he does expect us to listen to him.

The New Testament repeatedly depicts the disciples as people who *listen* to the Holy Spirit. Luke records Philip listening to the Spirit when prompted to witness to the Ethiopian eunuch, "And *the Spirit said* to Philip, 'Go over and join this chariot'" (Acts 8:29). Peter heeds the Spirit's direction when he recounts, "And *the Spirit told me* to go with them" (Acts 11:12). Paul remarks, "The *Holy Spirit testifies to me* in every city that imprisonment and afflictions await me" (Acts 20:23). And in Acts 15:28, the apostles and elders of the church sought the Spirit's wisdom, concluding they had discerned a decision that "seemed good to the Holy Spirit."

How could Philip, Peter, Paul, and the apostles and the elders of the Jerusalem church hear the Spirit if they were not intent on knowing him? Notice these sayings were not simply citations of Scripture, but fresh personal words meant for specific disciples in specific situations. Philip's prompt was not extended to everyone, nor Peter's invitation to visit Cornelius's home, and the Spirit's sobering promise of persecution in every city was made uniquely to Paul. Each one had a personal connection to the Holy Spirit.

Moreover, the Holy Spirit draws attention to himself through his various physical manifestations as a rushing wind, a pillar of cloud and fire, tongues of fire, and a dove. Does this detract from the Spirit's Christ-magnifying work? Not at all. As Sam Storms notes,

> The principal aim of the Spirit in what he does is to awaken us to the glory, splendor, and centrality of the work of Christ Jesus. But this does not mean that it is less than the Spirit at work when he awakens us also to his own glory and power and abiding presence. We should remember that the Holy

Spirit inspired hundreds of biblical passages that speak about himself and his work.

We are meant to know and heed the third person of the Trinity. The Spirit seeks not only to magnify Christ through us, but also to speak *to* us, prompting us throughout our life.

The Spirit seeks not only to magnify Christ through us, but also to speak *to* us, prompting us throughout our life.

8

Discerning Promptings

I WAS TALKING WITH someone one day who told me he had a prompting from the Spirit: God had told him to divorce his wife. I asked him why he felt he should divorce his wife. He had a number of reasons, but not one of them constituted biblical grounds for divorce. This was clearly not a prompting of the Spirit because the Spirit does not violate Scripture's teaching.

Discerning which thoughts are prompts from the Spirit and which are not can be challenging, especially when we have sinful motives. But even with good motives Scripture recognizes a degree of subjectivity in discerning the Holy Spirit's leading. Advising Gentile churches, the elders of the Jerusalem church wrote that "it has seemed good to the Holy Spirit" to give certain counsel (Acts 15:28). Regarding his instruction to widows who want to remarry that they are better off remaining single, Paul writes, "And I think that I too have the Spirit of God" (1 Cor 7:40). The only error-free source for the Spirit's speech is Scripture, and even that should be read carefully. Exploring the Spirit's more subjective communication, like prompts and prophecy, should be done with even more caution. We can use several "tests" to discern if our thoughts are actually from the Spirit.

THREE TESTS TO DISCERN THE SPIRIT'S VOICE
The Scripture Test
The Wisdom Test
The Ministry Test

DISCERNING THE SPIRIT'S LEADING

First, there is the *Scripture test.* In my experience, people sometimes confuse their own desires with the voice of the Holy Spirit. The husband I described earlier did just this. He should have used the Scripture test. If he had, it would have been clear that the Spirit had already spoken on the matter, and obeying him would have saved himself and his poor wife a lot of heartache. Whenever a so-called impression contradicts Scripture, always go with the Bible.

Then there is the *wisdom test.* Sometimes our impressions lack wisdom. It's not uncommon to hear people say the Holy Spirit told them to do something like quit their job while not having another source of income to support their family. When confronting this lack of wisdom I've heard various objections such as, "God will never let me down." Think about what would have happened if Jesus used similar reasoning when Satan tempted him with fame to jump off the highest point of the temple. However, instead of saying, "God will never let me down," Jesus said, "You shall not put the Lord your God to the test" (Lk 4:12). "God will never let me down" reasoning puts us—not God—in charge, treating him like a corporate sponsor for any wild-haired idea we may have. We use hyper-spiritual reasoning when we want God to endorse our agenda. In this case, it would have been wise to consider his wisdom in 1 Timothy 5:8, "If anyone does not provide for his relatives, and especially for members of his household, he has denied the faith and is worse than an unbeliever."

Zealous Christians sometimes say the Spirit is prompting them to sell their house and move to Africa for missions when they haven't even made a disciple in America. These "prompts" fail the *wisdom test*. While it's certainly possible for the Spirit to impress on us a change of job, home, or country, it's important we screen our impressions with wisdom. There is safety in an abundance of counselors (Prov 11:14), so make important decisions in community. Humbly seek out respected spiritual leaders before taking the leap.

Finally, there is the *ministry test*. Whenever we start a sentence with, "The Spirit told me . . ." we're on fallible ground. Nevertheless, the Bible does show us examples of people being *prompted* by the Holy Spirit to do various things. The interesting thing about these prompts is that they are typically ministry-minded things, like when the Spirit prompted Philip to witness to the Ethiopian eunuch, Peter to share the gospel with the household of Cornelius, and Paul to spread the gospel in various cities.

When I moved to a new city to plant a church, I had to office out of coffee shops the first few years. Occasionally, before I left the house or while I was driving, I would pray and ask the Holy Spirit to direct me to a coffee shop where I could meet people he was calling into the kingdom. Sometimes I would get the sense that I was supposed to go to a specific shop, and other times I wouldn't. When I did receive a prompt for a specific place, I often ended up having an evangelistic conversation with someone. Several of these turned into long-term relationships, with some of them coming to Christ. But there were also times when I ended up at a place and simply worked. I'd be willing to bet that just about any time we are prompted to share the gospel or meet a need, it's likely the Holy Spirit. This is the *ministry test*, evaluating a prompt based on a ministry orientation.

> Just about any time we are prompted to share the gospel or meet a need, it's likely the Holy Spirit.

THE PROPHETIC MINISTRY OF THE SPIRIT

Sometimes the Spirit speaks to us *prophetically*. There are various views on what prophecy is and how it functions in the church today. Few deny the prophetic role of the Spirit in the Old Testament, where God spoke regularly through his appointed prophets (Num 22:38; Deut 18:18-20; Ezek 2:7). What is debated is the role of the Spirit in speaking prophetically today in light of the New Testament. I will introduce three main views of what prophecy is and how it operates. Since prophecy is not a major focus in this book, I encourage you to study the topic further and discuss it with others, respectfully engaging with your church leaders.

The first view sees prophecy as speech that articulates something God spontaneously brings to mind or "reveals" to the speaker. This seems to have occurred in Acts 5 when Peter suddenly knows that Ananias is lying to him, and in John 4 when Jesus has on-the-spot insight into the Samaritan woman's marital history. However, this kind of spontaneous insight is not infallible for us; therefore, it can have mistakes and must be tested or evaluated according to Scripture (1 Cor 12:29; 1 Thess 5:19-21). Nevertheless, it can also serve to *exhort* others.

When I was twenty I went to Bible school overseas in part to recover from a really messed up relationship with my girlfriend back home. I was eager to turn things around, but on the first night a visiting speaker, whom I had never met, walked up to me and said, "You will not last the semester." Puzzled by what he said and why he said it, I blew it off and cruised through the semester, continuing to make bad decisions along the way. The second to last day of Bible school, I was caught making out with a woman in an off-limits room and was sent home. Looking back, I wonder what would have happened if I had heeded the speaker's warning. His spontaneous insight could have served as an exhortation to make more God-honoring decisions and get a lot more out of Bible school.

Prophecy can also *encourage*. In a particularly trying season of ministry, I was really fighting to find joy in Christ. I sensed the Lord's joy and struggled to do my best to preach well to my church. However, during this time I was bombarded by discouraging thoughts as I stepped up to preach. One particular Sunday, I sat down after preaching and experienced an unusual level of discouragement. After the service was over a woman whom I did not know walked up to me and said, "The Spirit wants you to know that your joy is your weapon." Then she walked away.

She had no knowledge of my internal struggle or how much that sentence meant to me. Her prophetic word strengthened me to continue to battle spiritual attacks and preach faithfully. Indeed, joy in our preaching and in our living is a tremendous instrument to deliver the truth of the gospel. These "prophecies" were the result of spontaneous insight and took the form of exhortation and encouragement. In fact, Paul says that all prophecy should build up, encourage, or console (1 Cor 14:3). It is others focused. The Spirit does these things in Scripture, and they can be very edifying to the people of God.

A second view sees prophecy as very similar to the gifts of preaching or teaching, which has ample support in the New Testament (1 Cor 14:1-40; Acts 2:14-41; 19:8-10; Rom 12:6; 1 Thess 5:19-21; 1 Tim 1:18). We sometimes experience this ministry of the Holy Spirit when hearing the Scriptures preached or taught. It is that feeling that "the preacher is speaking right to me," when it is actually the Spirit quickening our heart and mind to something. It is the person of the Spirit speaking to us through a Scripture-guided person in the flesh. It need not be flashy, but when it happens we should pay attention and respond.

In an extremely difficult season of my life I was brought to my knees, crying out for God to deliver me. Through tears I lifted my arms and pleaded with God to pull me out of my sinking circumstances. Within minutes my wife received a message from a friend who said she felt like the Holy Spirit was telling her to tell me that, like Peter who sank when walking on the water with Jesus (Mt 14:28-32), Jesus was extending his hand to me and was going to pull me up. The parallel imagery was uncanny, and the hope that traveled through those words into my heart was incredibly comforting. Shortly after this, I received a phone call that led to a radical change of circumstances. The Spirit spoke through two people to supernaturally lift me out of despair and deliver me from awful circumstances.

As a preacher and teacher, I sometimes experience this kind of prophecy. I manuscript my sermons but always ask the Holy Spirit to grant prophetic power to what I say, inviting him to make on-the-spot edits. The Spirit always gets the final revision. Sometimes while I am preaching an image or phrase will appear in my mind that I had not written down or considered before. Very often I will choose to share that image or wording, and sometimes people will comment on how helpful that particular, spontaneous change was. Sometimes I don't receive any feedback at all. Other times I will hear about how helpful the spontaneous change was weeks or even months later. Regardless, it's important to note that prophetic experience does not make a preacher or teacher more valuable.

The Holy Spirit is also at work through our hard-won messages and lessons, electrifying the Word of God in the hearts of his people. We must not strive for prophecy but for faithfulness to God's infallible, holy, transforming Word: "For the word of God is living and active, sharper than any two-edged sword, piercing to the division of soul and of spirit, of joints and of marrow, and discerning the thoughts and intentions of the heart" (Heb 4:12). The Word is *the* prophetic message from God to us. We should always lean in when Scripture is read, prayed, taught, preached, or counseled.

> All prophecy should be used to build up, encourage, and comfort the people of God.

A third view sees prophecy as speaking with words equal in authority to the Old Testament prophets and New Testament apostles. It is difficult to find support for this view in the New Testament itself. In summary, all prophecy should be used to build up, encourage, and comfort the people of God, *not* to leverage for personal worth or to exercise spiritual power over others (1 Cor 14:3). Prophecy should also be used to draw attention to God and his remarkable grace toward us in Jesus, not seek to bring attention to ourselves.

Any healthy relationship relies on two-way communication. Discerning prompts and prophecy is one way, the result of listening to the Spirit. What does it look like to respond to him? We turn to that next.

Praying in the Spirit

IN THE FILM *Braveheart*, Stephen, an Irish warrior who fights with William Wallace, periodically bursts aloud as though talking with an invisible person. This prompts one of the men to ask, "Is your father a ghost or do you converse with the Almighty?" Stephen responds, "In order to find his equal, an Irishman is forced to talk to God." They nickname him "The Madman." Is this what conversing with the Spirit looks like—walking around like a blabbering madman?

Paul recognizes the importance of a dynamic relationship with the Spirit when he concludes his second letter to the church at Corinth saying, "The grace of the Lord Jesus Christ and the love of God *and the fellowship of the Holy Spirit* be with you all" (2 Cor 13:14; see also Phil 2:1). What does fellowship with the Holy Spirit look like?

PRAYING TO THE SPIRIT

Whenever I suggest praying to the Spirit, I occasionally hear the objection that the Bible does not tell us to pray to the Spirit, only to the Father or the Son. This objection is similar to what's called a word-thing fallacy. Just because the precise words aren't in the Bible, doesn't mean the thing isn't theologically or practically valid. The Bible doesn't tell us a lot of things outright, such as to memorize Scripture, yet no one would dispute the value of memorizing the Bible. Bible memorization is a practical implication of the Scripture's self-attesting worth, but it is not a rule. Similarly, the word *Trinity* does not appear in the Bible, yet we use it to describe what is theologically present in the Scriptures. Praying to the Holy Spirit, then, is an implication of his being a person within the Trinity.

John Piper underscores this when he describes the importance of apologizing to the Spirit if we have grieved the Spirit: "I mean, it is just strange if he is a person and I have grieved him that I would just ignore talking to him and go to the Father and say: I am sorry I grieved your Spirit." He concludes, "Realize that Jesus and the Holy Spirit are persons and to speak to them as a saved sinner would, cannot be unnatural." Now, is this a rule? Perhaps not. But like Bible memorization, if we don't pray to and in the Spirit, we're missing out. In my experience the more you come to know the Spirit, the more you find yourself talking to him. Of course, there are no prayer sidebars: when we pray to one person of the Trinity, the rest overhear.

As Stanley Hauerwas and William Willimon point out, the historical service of ordination includes a prayer to the Spirit, "Come, Creator Spirit." It is fitting for someone setting out to shepherd the flock of God to begin with a prayer of helplessness to the all-powerful Helper. Of course, as St. Augustine demonstrates in his prayer to the Spirit, we all need the Spirit's help:

> Breathe in me, O Holy Spirit, that my thoughts may all be holy.
> Act in me, O Holy Spirit, that my work, too, may be holy.

Draw my heart, O Holy Spirit, that I love but what is holy.
Strengthen me, O Holy Spirit, to defend all that is holy.
Guard me, then, O Holy Spirit, that I always may be
holy. Amen.

After teaching his disciples to pray, Jesus exhorts them to sedulously
seek the Father, promising them the heavenly Father will "give the
Holy Spirit to those who ask him" (Lk 11:13). Commenting on this
verse, John Owen writes, "The promise of bestowing the Spirit is
accompanied with a prescription of duty unto us, *that we should
ask him or pray for him.*" Jesus reminds us that we are to continually
seek the Spirit, asking for his presence and power for life and
godliness. Although prayers to the Spirit are commonplace in
church history, we should consider Scripture's instruction to pray
"in the Spirit" (Jude 20; see also Eph 6:18). Before explaining what
that looks like, it will be helpful to consider how *not* to pray in
the Spirit.

THE DIFFICULTY OF PRAYER

Like communication in any relationship, prayer can be difficult and
ungratifying. Sometimes I have to force myself to pray. Other times
I am easily distracted in prayer. When we pray "in" our doctrine,
in emotion, or in a list, we often fail to pray in the Spirit. Praying
in our doctrine is praying with the ultimate aim of being theologically accurate. The focus devolves into doctrinal precision over
heartfelt devotion. Spoken prayers, especially ones scripted for public
delivery, often face this danger. If we're not careful, we can begin
praying in a way that brings attention to our words, not out of
personal attentiveness to the Father, Son, and Holy Spirit. Jesus
cautions us of praying for show, which is often marked by an

abundance of words or a posture for attention (Mt 6:7). This kind of prayer is before others instead of with God.

In fact, sometimes the Spirit doesn't even use words; he groans (Rom 8:26). This happens when we are moved over a truth, not when we're meticulously arranging the truth. I've noticed young men often face this particular struggle. I certainly did! We tend to pray good theology instead of letting good theology pray. When we pray good theology, we strive to word everything as though writing a systematic theology. It comes out doctrinally accurate but relationally cold. But when good theology prays us, we simply relate to God out of sincere belief and heartfelt trust, as we would a respected friend.

> We tend to pray good theology instead of letting good theology pray.

Another way we miss praying in the Spirit is by praying *in a list*. This kind of prayer is more mechanical than relational, like going through steps or ticking things off a grocery list. It can even happen when we are praying the Lord's Prayer or using a prayer book. While the Lord certainly wants to hear our requests, he is not a grocer and he does not have things for sale. He is our Father who loves to give good gifts and sent his Spirit into our hearts to help us pray (Mt 7:9-11). We do better to yield to the Spirit in our praying, following his prompts as we meditate on God's Word or pray for others.

> **THREE WAYS WE MISS PRAYING IN THE SPIRIT**
> Praying in Doctrine
> Praying in a List
> Praying in Emotion

We may also fall into praying *in emotion*. The emotional pray-er looks more for an experience than for God. How do you know if this is you? You tend to judge your prayer time based on how emotionally stirred you are. If you feel something, you've done a good job, but if you or someone else who is praying hasn't moved the emotions, then that's bad praying. It's okay if your prayers sometimes lack emotion, or if all you can do is get just a few words out. One of the most frequent prayers in the Bible is, "Lord, have mercy" (Deut 30:3; Ps 25:6; 123:3; Hab 3:2; Mt 15:22; 17:15; 20:30). However, the Lord is certainly worthy of affection-stirring prayers that reflect his immensity and grace.

PRAYING IN THE SPIRIT

What then is praying in the Spirit? Simply put, praying in the Spirit means *praying in his presence, with his direction, and in his power*. When we pray in his presence, we enjoy his fellowship, as we saw earlier. But praying in the Spirit can also mean seeking his guidance. The Spirit may also intensify our prayers with powerful effect. We can address the Spirit directly as a full person of the Trinity by following his lead in prayer and trusting in his power.

Ephesians 6:17-18 exhorts us to take up "the sword of the Spirit, which is the word of God, praying at all times in the Spirit, with all prayer and supplication." With spiritual war raging around us, all too often we stand frozen in fear or indifference, our sword resting idly in the corner. Instead we should pray to the person of the Spirit with Scripture as our guide. For example, since the Spirit is the Helper, I often pray to him for help: "Holy Spirit, help me flee the temptations I often face, of pride, vanity, and lust." Then I follow the prayer with a Scripture, such as, "Flee youthful passions and pursue righteousness, faith, love, and peace, along with those

who call on the Lord from a pure heart" (2 Tim 2:22). Or if I want
to experience communion with God, I will pray, "Spirit, you search
out all things, even the depths of God, so guide me into the depths
of his presence" (based on 1 Cor 2:10). Informal prayers are great
too. If I am at a loss for what to pray or where to go in life I will
pray, "Holy Spirit, I don't know what's next; I need you to guide
me. Will you show me what the Father wants?" And when we lack
the words, the Spirit will groan on our behalf (Rom 8:26).

Praying in the Spirit includes praying in his power, not our own.
As Origen put it, the Spirit "intensifies the petition." We may
experience this intensification when we are praying silently or out
loud, which lends a kind of power to the prayer that is very edifying
for the saints. When I gather with those who are serving our church
each Sunday to pray, there are often moments when the power of
the Spirit is felt. Sometimes people will pray exact things that are
in my sermon manuscript without knowing it. Other times fresh
prayers for God's work among us and for our city pulse with
spiritual power. When this happens, it's as if the Holy Spirit is
waving a banner over us saying, "I am with you and this is what
I want."

Powerful prayer is not necessarily emotional or loud or the result
of a single charismatic cry. The Spirit's power often works through
the persistent. When Elijah prayed it would not rain, God stopped
the rains for three and a half years. How did Elijah pray? Earnestly.
Commenting on this kind of prayer James says, "The prayer of a
righteous person is powerful and effective" (Jas 5:16-17 NIV).
Teaching his disciples to pray and not give up, Jesus told a parable
that praised the widow who continually pestered the judge for
justice (Lk 18:1-11). Hang in there. Pray often. Be righteous. But
be careful to put your hope in God, not in prayer. Yield to him

always and you will be blessed by the Spirit, enjoying his life and peace. Praying in the Spirit means praying in his presence, which includes following his direction and depending on his power.

> Be careful to put your hope in God, not in prayer.

Charismatic scholar Gordon Fee has noted that much of what passes for praying in the Spirit often misses the mark because it severs prayer from the mission of God. When Paul gave this instruction to the Ephesians, it was with the advance of the gospel in view. Fee writes, "Praying in the Spirit is not only so that people will be able to withstand the enemy's onslaught, but so that Paul will be enabled to carry the gospel forward." Prayer is not merely for the "holy huddle" but for the renewal of the world. Let's not forget to pray asking the Spirit to open the eyes of our friends, co-workers, neighbors, and family members to the magnificence of Christ. Plead with the Spirit to continue redeeming and perfecting all creation.

A final way to pray in the Spirit is, as Martin Luther put it, to "let your thoughts take you for a walk." What did he mean? Sometimes I get stuck praying a list and I don't allow myself to veer onto the scenic drive to take in unplanned sights of God's glory, beauty, truth, and goodness. Remembering I need to let the Spirit take my thoughts for a walk has been very freeing for me in prayer. It has enabled me to soak in the wonder of God, linger over some truth about his character, or contemplate a phrase in his Word.

I used to feel guilty when I departed from my list because I would run out of time to pray for others, but God has freed me from that by reminding me of the ultimate goal of enjoying his presence. I find myself "veering off" when I pray aloud or by myself.

When I'm out and about walking in my neighborhood or on a trail, I will simply talk to God as though he is walking beside me. Onlookers may confuse me with a madman!

Praying in the Spirit—rather than in a doctrine, list, or emotion— is a wonderful way to cultivate communion with God and enjoy his fellowship. Unlike the father we encountered in the story at the beginning of chapter seven, we need not construct ceremonies out of thin air and breathe on them for meaning. Instead, the Holy Spirit has breathed new life into us and given us meaning in his fellowship and mission.

10

Mission with the Wind

WE'RE TOLD THAT God added daily to the church in Acts. I'm confident he's still doing the same today. Somewhere in the world people are saved into God's new community every single day. The last statistic I read put conversions in Africa at about nine thousand a day.

When I was in Uganda in the summer of 2010, we crammed into an open-air brick building in a remote village to preach the gospel and teach the Scriptures. The building was packed. Sensing the need for more Bibles, we sent a team member by motorcycle to the closest city to get more copies in their dialect. After our team member returned and the teaching time was done, we announced that we would be distributing Bibles in their language. Although we had formed a line to give them away, the entire room rushed to the front. Desperate to have their own Bibles, the students cried out for joy, piling onto one another, with smiles stretched as wide as their arms to receive the Scriptures.

In 1900 Nigeria's Christian population was 180,000. By 2050 it is projected to be 180 million. Nigerian Christians promote the faith through various entrepreneurial methods, including videos that spread the message of Christianity quickly.

Missiologists credit the explosive growth in Africa to the abundant presence of charismatics, who emphasize the power and presence of the Holy Spirit. This reminds us that the Spirit saves us not only *into* the church but also *onto* his mission. He is eager to work through us like he worked through the early church, compelling us to tell of "the mighty works of God" (Acts 2:11).

A GOSPEL BREEZE

With the "fire and wind" in us, we might expect mission to be marked by otherworldly miracles, radical conversions, and epic acts of justice and mercy. That does happen, but on the back of ordinary obedience, slow conversion, and reluctant mercy ministry. Most days aren't spectacular.

Mission can be boring, mundane, ordinary. I wake up, exercise, try to listen to the Spirit, and eat my breakfast, attempting to remind my family and myself that God is the most important person in our day without getting frustrated that my six-year-old isn't paying attention. In the chaos of packing lunches and tying shoelaces, goading my children into the car with sharp reminders that we need to be on time, I often forget that one of them is a sinner estranged from God. Mission is there, looking at me from across the breakfast table, awaiting ordinary obedience from a very imperfect father. And she is one in a neighborhood of hundreds and a city of millions.

A cursory reading of any New Testament document leaves the impression that the "good news" was so good people had to get it out. The stories of conversion, the commissions of Jesus, the prompts of the Spirit to witness or plant a church, the reminders to walk with outsiders in wisdom and grace, the eagerness for the gospel to go to places unknown. It all jumps off the page. The letters themselves are proof: circular epistles intended to promote the gospel in and through the church.

The holy Wind is not meant to stop at the door of the church, but to blow right through us into the lives of others. But the more disconnected we become from the Spirit, the more sharing the good news feels like a task, an event, something to check off the Christian to-do list. As a result, we become more mechanical in our witness, trying to force the word *Jesus* into a conversation or absconding with gospel to build doctrinal or spiritual towers around ourselves.

> The holy Wind is not meant to stop at the door of the church, but to blow right through us into the lives of others.

Some of our neighbors got to know the owner of a bar on Rainey Street, a strip of homes converted into boutique night clubs. They asked if they could bring him to our church. I thought it was kind of weird because I knew they attended another church, but then they explained their church would be too wild for him, that he wouldn't feel comfortable there. Another friend of mine often says he's glad he knows me so he can send all his non-Christian skeptic and artist friends to our church since they wouldn't feel at home as his church. Our neighbors felt like their church was too consumed with spiritual experiences to be relevant to a seeker, and our other friends knew their church would speak in a language their secular friends wouldn't understand. Both of them felt they couldn't introduce their spiritually curious friends to their own communities.

Perhaps they were mistaken, perhaps not. Either way, it's so easy for churches to get off the mission of God by focusing on experiences and doctrine, gatherings and classes. After becoming a Christian, it's like we hang a "Do not disturb" sign on the door, telling the Holy Spirit he is no longer allowed in, not permitted to blow through us for witness. Maybe this is because nailing our doctrine and getting lost in emotion are easier; they don't require anything of us. They minimize the risk of losing face or losing friends. Or maybe we just love "spiritual" comfort. Whatever it is, we need to topple the walls and ask—implore—the Holy Spirit to blow through us again.

As our little church began to break bread and lines of privacy, we began to cross yet another line, the invisible boundary between the church and the city, which separated Christian and not Christian. It began in prayer for our city, where our hearts were changed by the Spirit of God. Seeking to give life, not take life, from the city, we looked around and asked two questions: Where is the city broken? What would it look like for the gospel to address the brokenness of the city? The only way to answer these questions honestly was to rub shoulders with fellow citizens, neighbors, and coworkers. We met them on common cultural ground—in bars, restaurants, cinemas, shelters, at work, and on the street. Very slowly the line became blurred between sinner and saint. We too were learning to be friends of sinners. We began to practice honesty about our need for a Redeemer alongside the not yet redeemed. Punching holes in the holier-than-thou boundary, the broken citizens of our city began to trickle into our community and hear the good news of Jesus.

The Spirit is intent on creating this kind of community, where all kinds of people are welcome, Christian or not. Like in Acts 2, he wants to give us favor with all the people (Acts 2:47). Like in Acts 5, this requires line-erasing honesty and confession and a reconfiguring of our expectations around Jesus. After the Ananias and Sapphira episode, we're told that "more than ever believers were added to the Lord, multitudes of both men and women" (Acts 5:14). This was accompanied by miraculous acts and immediate persecution and imprisonment. Joining the Spirit in mission will cost you, but the loss is eclipsed by the reward.

> Joining the Spirit in mission will cost you, but the loss is eclipsed by the reward.

SLOW CONVERSION

Conversions don't happen as quickly as I want them to. Typically, conversion is slow, not sudden. While the rescue of someone out of darkness into light is a seismic spiritual event, the magnitude of conversion is not always accompanied by spectacular signs. Mike was the manager of one of my favorite coffee shops. We hit it off and soon began connecting outside of the coffee shop. One afternoon over coffee he told me about his church wounds. After he finished his story, he leaned across the table and said, "Will your church disappoint me?" I paused to think. I knew it would, so I replied, "Yes, our church will disappoint you, but we will do our best to point you to the Savior who doesn't."

We continued to connect off and on, talking about the deep things of life, but I saw no substantive change in his life. It was clear to me that, while knowledgeable about Christianity, he lacked a true understanding of grace and that his church experience had led to deep cynicism. Three years later, after he'd moved away with his girlfriend, he sent me an email to thank me for telling him he lacked an understanding of grace and that my words had stuck with him, sometimes moving him closer to who he really is and who God is. A couple years later, he moved back to Austin and reached out. He began to attend church occasionally and connected with one of the leaders. Engaged to a New Age artist, whom he admired deeply, he found it difficult to explain and navigate his growing spiritual convictions.

Five years after our first meeting, he joined a group of curious and skeptical people who met in our home to discuss big challenges to Christian faith. There he confessed he did not know if he was Christian or not, though the Christian system of belief possessed a flawless logic to him. Several months later, he sent me a note saying, "I'm hoping for a spot where I, a believer in Jesus, and someone like my fiancée, a nonbeliever, can come together to talk about the things in existence that we all struggle with. What y'all made was just that." Something happened over those five years; it was gradual, not dramatic. His beliefs were tested and refined within an accepting community that prized the truth of the gospel. At times I was tempted to write him off as forever hardened to the hope of Christ, but the Spirit was there all along, silently at work in ways I could not see. I could recount many more stories of slow conversion. The Spirit is often subtle, not showy, as he moves the kingdom forward.

RELUCTANT MERCY AND JUSTICE

The Spirit also compels us to show mercy and overturn injustice. As God's people we are to do justice, love mercy, and walk humbly with God (Mic 6:8; 1 Jn 3:17). In the words of Jesus, we are to love our neighbor (Mt 19:19). Who is our neighbor? In the parable of the merciful Samaritan, Jesus shows us our neighbor is the person in need (Lk 10:25-37). What does mercy do for them? This parable shows us that mercy feels, acts, and sacrifices. The Samaritan did not pass to the other side of his neighbor's need. He *felt* pity and drew near. Then he *acted* by binding up his wounds, presumably with his own clothing since the man was left naked. He applies antiseptic (wine) and a painkiller (oil) and could have left him there, but instead he *sacrificed* his time and comfort by putting the man on his own animal, which meant he had to walk the rest of the way. Then he brought him to an inn and cared for him, paying for about a two-week stay. Mercy gives to such an extent that it hurts. It is sacrificial. Mercy feels, acts, and sacrifices.

Although mercy is a gift given to some people, mercy is for all people and should blow through all of us. This is the point of Jesus' parable. The answer to the question "Who is my neighbor?" is "the one in need." Jesus then concludes, "You go, and do likewise" (Lk 10:37). While the measure of mercy differs from person to person, the Spirit is given without measure (Jn 3:34). A maturing Christian will grow in her expression of God's mercy over time.

In his helpful book *Ministries of Mercy*, Tim Keller simplifies mercy as "meeting needs through deeds." Now does that mean we sell everything we have and give it to the poor, jeopardizing our own family? No. Keller says that when a desire (compassion), an opportunity (person on the ground), and ability (resources) are present there is a call to show mercy. Mercy meets needs and loves neighbors. But mercy doesn't solve the problem. Justice solves the problem. Mercy helps the person on the street for a moment, but justice gets him off the street for a lifetime. Mercy helps the wounded man, but justice runs out all the thieves so there are fewer muggings and deaths. Justice appoints a soldier patrol and captures criminals. God calls us to both mercy and justice, equipping the church with gifts to help us move forward. As the Spirit blows through God's new community, the church becomes a counter-cultural expression of the city to come, where righteousness and justice dwell.

> Mercy helps the person on the street for a moment, but justice gets him off the street for a lifetime.

While I am both convicted and inspired by the parable of the Good Samaritan, I sometimes feel a disinterest in mercy when opportunity and ability present themselves. At least once a month, I have the opportunity to love our poor neighbors in the government housing next to our neighborhood. We set up a monthly community event, where we partner with them to cook hotdogs, play games, and connect. Almost every time the event rolls around, I have to talk myself into going. Others who participate encounter similar challenges. In fact, a lot of the middle-class people in our church soon get frustrated that we aren't "accomplishing something." The impulse to be productive, to measure impact, and in some cases to offload guilt, prevents people from entering into simple, repeated acts of mercy. Perhaps this is also because we are so inexperienced in showing mercy in our everyday relationships.

As people vent their frustrations in community, we are able to pastor them into the inherent value of showing God's mercy, as well as educate them on the benefits of faithful presence, mentoring, and conversations that further racial reconciliation. Those who press through these challenges and continue to show up get to witness the Spirit's work. We've seen a neglected child get adopted, the ailing elderly visited in hospitals, bitter married couples counseled, residents moved into new apartments, employment gained, and much more. But on the face of it, our community event is not impressive. We will not win any awards or become a case study for successful mercy ministry, but we will be there, sometimes reluctantly, because of the subtle prompting of the Holy Spirit, as we move toward the sacred and just city of God.

11

Experiencing the Power

WHEN BILL MARIS, founder of Google Ventures, decided to build a company that cured death some people sneered, but others pulled out their wallets. In 2013 Google launched Calico (California Life Company) with a billion dollars in funding to succeed in their mission of transcending death and preserving consciousness. Maris is in cahoots with Ray Kurzweil, the futurist who popularized the notion of the *singularity*—the idea that humans will merge with artificial intelligence to transcend biological limitations (think *Ghost in the Shell*). These so-called immortalists are dead serious about their ventures. Take Brian Hanley, a sixty-year-old microbiologist who injected himself with the growth hormone GHRH. He experienced increased strength, sharper eyesight, and better cholesterol levels. Hanley also herniated a disc trying to lift a refrigerator. Apparently the growth hormone went to his head! Kurzweil believes that by the 2030s we will be injecting ourselves with nanobots to repair the body and the brain. Shortly thereafter, nanobots will connect our brains to the cloud and our intelligence will multiply rapidly, making us like gods.

The pursuit of immortality is understandable given humanity's beleaguered history with disease, famine, and death. Who wouldn't want to undo that? Unfortunately, immortalist research overlooks the cause of death—sin—and bypasses the real cure—the Redeemer—lowering their objective to self-deification. Alternatively, if we walk in step with the Holy Spirit, we will eventually take on the properties of the ultimate human: "Just as we have borne the image of the man of dust, we shall also bear the image of the man of heaven" (1 Cor 15:49). This transformation, however, requires faith in Jesus, not "faith-based tech."

One day our transformation will be so pure and so thorough that not only will the body be purified but also the soul. Sinful desires associated with our broken world will no longer be present in us. Not a single motive will be tainted. Heart, body, and mind will burst with the radiance of Christ, each person refracting his glory through their own unique personality and gifting. This diverse, expansive manifestation of the glory of God in humans is what led St. Irenaeus to describe the glory of God as "man fully alive." He insists, "The life of man consists in beholding God." If this is our future, our life aim should not be to cure death (that is God's work) but to close the gap on the heavenly man by beholding the image of the Son (Rom 8:29). In short, keeping in step with the Spirit puts us on track to look like Jesus.

THE POWER OF THE SPIRIT

So far I have tried to make a strong case for relating to the Spirit as a person. However, it is important we not put the personality of the Spirit at odds with the power of the Spirit. In fact, Jesus' life and ministry reveal the Spirit is not merely a person to befriend but a power to rely on.

The Gospel of Luke begins with Jesus being conceived under the generative flutter of the Spirit: "The angel answered her, 'The Holy Spirit will come upon you, and the power of the Most High will overshadow you; therefore the child to be born will be called holy—the Son of God'" (Lk 1:35). Reminiscent of the Sprit's hovering activity throughout the Old Testament, the Spirit's power opens a portal for the divine Son of God to inhabit the womb of Mary.

> The Spirit is not merely a person to befriend but a power to rely on.

The Spirit continued to hover around Jesus as he entered the temple for dedication. There the Spirit moved powerfully in Simeon and Anna, stirring them to announce Jesus as the long-awaited Messiah. After this announcement Jesus continued to grow in wisdom and stature, but two things occurred before he began his public ministry. First, Jesus was baptized, where he heard the voice of the Father and saw a manifestation of the Spirit descending on him as a dove. The Spirit marked Jesus for a ministry which John the Baptist announced would entail Jesus baptizing people "with the Holy Spirit and fire" (Lk 3:16). The person and power of the Spirit pulsed through Jesus' early years.

Next the Holy Spirit compelled Jesus to enter the wilderness, where he faced Satan's temptations: "Jesus, *full of the Holy Spirit*, returned from the Jordan and was *led by the Spirit* in the wilderness for forty days, being tempted by the devil" (Lk 4:1-2). The Spirit empowered Jesus to dismantle Satan's devices, triumphing where Israel had failed in the past. As a result, Jesus' forty days prove him to be the one true Israelite who would redeem Israel's forty years of wilderness wanderings. Jesus makes a "second exodus" possible through his ministry, life, death, and resurrection. He does this, not on his own, but in reliance on the Spirit. Emerging from the wilderness, Jesus returns to Galilee to begin his ministry in "the power of the Spirit" and was praised by all (Lk 4:14-15). Saturated in images of the Spirit, Luke's Gospel leads us to the unmistakable conclusion that Jesus relied on the power and presence of the Holy Spirit for everything he did.

Observing Jesus' reliance on the Holy Spirit could raise some questions about Jesus' inherent power and ability to conduct his ministry and life. Does his reliance on the Spirit subtract from Jesus' deity? Bruce Ware clarifies:

> What could the Spirit of God contribute to the *deity* of Christ? Nothing! As God he possesses everything infinitely, and nothing can be added to him.... What could the Spirit of God contribute to the *humanity* of Christ? The answer is: everything of supernatural power and enablement that he, in his human nature, would lack. The only way to make sense, then, of the fact that Jesus came in the power of the Spirit is to understand that he lived his life fundamentally as a man, and as such, he relied on the Spirit to provide the power, grace, knowledge, wisdom, direction, and enablement he needed, moment by moment and day by day.

As it turns out, Jesus is our example not only of the ultimate human but also of humble reliance on the Holy Spirit!

FILLING WITH THE SPIRIT

What, then, does it look like for us to be filled with that same Spirit? The filling of the Spirit is not a *one-time event* but a *recurring experience* of spiritual empowerment for growth and ministry. Being filled with the Spirit should not be confused with "baptism in the Spirit," which is a one-time event where we are initially indwelt with the Spirit and joined with the saints as part of the body of Christ (1 Cor 12:13). Although we are indwelt with the person of the Spirit (or *regenerated*) at a single point in time, our experience of his power can go up and down. We can quench the Spirit (Eph 4:30; 1 Thess 5:19) or be emboldened by the Spirit (1 Cor 12:11). Paul exhorts us to "be filled with the Spirit" (Eph 5:18).

For example, although the disciples experienced a filling of the Spirit at Pentecost, the book of Acts records them being filled over and over again in various contexts for different ministries. In Acts 4:8, Peter again is "filled with the Holy Spirit" to preach to Jewish religious leaders. A similar experience occurs with Stephen, a man "full of the Spirit and of wisdom" (Acts 6:3), who is freshly filled with the Spirit to endure persecution in witness to the risen Jesus (Acts 7:55). Paul was filled with the Holy Spirit in Acts 9:17, but then filled again with the Spirit to rebuke a magician who was interfering with Paul's evangelism (Acts 13:9). Filling is intermittent and continual.

Filling with the Holy Spirit also produces spiritual growth, producing increased understanding, wisdom, joy, hope, and peace (Col 1:9; Acts 13:52; Rom 15:13). Therefore, we should seek the continual filling of the Holy Spirit to be emboldened to share the gospel, enjoy God's presence, and make Christ-honoring decisions. For this reason, Paul repeatedly prays for churches to be filled with the Holy Spirit (Rom 15:13; Col 1:9).

In the movie *Limitless*, the central character stumbles upon some pills that allow him to use one hundred percent of his brain. When he is on the pills, he is able to solve complex math equations, write a book in four days, and learn foreign languages in hours. I wonder what would happen if we used one hundred percent of the Holy Spirit? Perhaps it's a crude analogy, but it does make you wonder—why don't we experience more of the Spirit's power?

ALTERNATIVE POWER SUPPLIES

In hydroelectricity, power is generated by a flowing body of water. When the water flows, there is plenty of power, but when the water slows or stops the electric power declines. One reason we do not experience more of the Spirit's power is that we fill up on other things, alternative power sources, which quench the Spirit. Three common alternative sources are reason, emotion, and experience.

Western Christians are particularly susceptible to substituting the Holy Spirit with *reason*. This often surfaces when we are faced with temptation. For example, when an attractive person walks by or pops up on our screen, we have a decision to make. We can appreciate their beauty and move on or linger in envious comparison or degrading lust. In that moment we often choose to enter an inner dialogue with our reason, missing the presence of the Spirit. We think to ourselves, "I know I shouldn't linger. The Bible tells me that love does not envy (1 Cor 13:4) or to flee lust and pursue righteousness (2 Tim 2:22). I know Jesus is better, but oh well, I'm gonna go ahead and look more." Powerless to overcome envy or lust, we cave into the temptation, spinning away from the peace of Christ. In this example, reason functions as an alternate power supply because it displaces the voice of the Spirit. We mistake the voice of the Spirit for the voice of reason. What would happen if in the moment we simply recognized our thoughts as the living Spirit's prompt to seek Christ. Instead of carrying on with our moral and spiritual reasoning, temptation would transform into a moment of communion! In my experience, introducing a "third person" into temptation by simply acknowledging the Spirit's presence and my thoughts as his prompts helps tremendously.

This alternate power supply can hum when we are switched on to identifying personal idols. I love a clean house, my wife loves piles, and the children love a mess. After we had our first child, I had to learn how to help clean the house, but then we had a second child, and a third, and it became impossible for my wife to keep up. One day I was doing housework and my wife confronted me, telling me she felt judged by the way I was cleaning. I was, in fact, frustrated that I had to clean. I was judging her for not getting it done. Negative vibes radiated from me like Magneto's destructive magnetic fields. Saddened by the effect of my sin on my wife, I reflected on what was motivating my judgment. Eventually, I realized it was the idol of control.

I tend to believe that if I can secure a clean house, when I come home from a long day at work I will be able to experience peace. I needed the Prince of Peace to topple the idol of control. Instead of expecting tidiness to soothe my weary heart, I needed to turn to Jesus during work, and on the way home from work, to ask for the peace of Christ to rule my heart (Col 3:15), not the endless longing for control. I confessed my sin to the Lord, received his forgiveness, and sought to substitute Jesus for control. But I still found myself cleaning out of anger. I was powerless to change. It wasn't enough to analyze my idolatrous motivations and match them with superior gospel truths.

In this process, I had not once acknowledged the presence of the Holy Spirit, who was revealing all of this to me and inviting me into repentant change. I had mistaken my analysis for his voice! Once I realized this, I confessed it to the Lord and asked for the Spirit's power to change. I began to recognize that my awareness of sin, and the superiority of Jesus, was something the Holy Spirit was showing me. Slowly I began to change, cleaning without the vibes, until one day I told my wife, "I don't want you to worry about having the house clean every day. God has given you gifts that would be better used elsewhere." Oh, and hiring an occasional house cleaner certainly helped!

The temptation to rely on pure reason is reinforced in our society every single day. From the moment we wake up, our phones extend the promise of salvation through mastery of information. If I can stay on top of world events, stay abreast of what my friends are doing, get through my calendared meetings, and tick off the Evernote list, then I'll have meaning and experience satisfaction. If something goes south with our health, we look to a thorough medical diagnosis and a treatment plan for peace.

We frequently seek deliverance from our circumstances and sorrows by faith in *comprehensive explanations*. We tend to believe that if we can master the ins and outs of our difficulties and pain, the explanation will set us free. I see this in counseling quite frequently. A person will come to me with a gnawing sense of restlessness, poor self-image, or despair. As I counsel them, it becomes apparent they believe if they can understand their relational hurts, painful family experiences, and flawed genetic inheritance, *they will be free*. This surfaces in the woman who thinks if she can identify all the negative influences in her life for who she's become, she will be free from her depression. Or the man who shows up to community group with his sin so thoroughly analyzed, his idolatry broken down into fine detail, that people think there's nothing to say. In both of these cases, comprehensive explanations of life influences and sinful patterns have subverted simple, Spirit-empowered prompts to repentance and faith in the promises of God. It can also minimize personal responsibility and sideline wise counsel and prayer from others.

While understanding our stressors, negative influences, and painful experiences can be part of the process of healing, it is never the cure. The brute fact is that we will never be able to comprehend the totality of the complex and varied influences on our lives. Only an omniscient God can do that, and most of the time, in his mercy, he chooses not to reveal all of this to us. Instead, he extends us relief in his promise to hear our simple cry, "Lord have mercy." In response, he sends his Comforter into our hearts, who assures us that the Lord understands our weakness and has done something decisive about it. He has severed the power of sin and given us the power of the Spirit to walk by faith in a Redeemer who accepts and loves us in a way we could never love or accept ourselves. His love transcends the failure of our friends, parents, and churches and frees us to pass on his love, forgiving just as we have been forgiven (Eph 4:32). In brief, self-understanding is no salvation. Self-analysis and finely tuned idolatry leave us trapped inside the idol. Introspective journeys that relocate blame can quickly become dead-end roads.

> We will never be able to comprehend the totality of the complex and varied influences on our lives. Only an omniscient God can do that.

There is only one person who understands you completely, who sees everything, and knows the complex experience of pain, joy, failure, and shame. The Father, Son, and Holy Spirit know and search out all things—the things we hide and the things we do not see. The secret sins and the invisible ones. God sees all the things that, if we were to see at once, would crush us. But instead of crushing us with his omniscience, Jesus is crushed by it. The weight of sin and the gravity of evil are heaped on the flawless, innocent Son of God, who atones for our sin, guilt, and shame and rises victorious over sin, death, and hell. As a result, the Father can say with full-throated affection, "I love you." Jesus is the shimmering proof of the liberating love of God: "In this is love, not that we have loved God but that he loved us and sent his Son to be the propitiation for our sins" (1 Jn 4:10). Without the Holy Spirit, that proof remains lodged in our cerebral cortex. Fortunately, the Spirit travels through spiritual truths, even when we don't comprehend them fully, to embed the wondrous love of God in our hearts.

Another alternative power supply is *emotion*. At the end of a day someone will likely ask us, "How was your day?" We typically respond out of emotion. If we *feel* like it was a "good" day, we will say it was good or great. If we feel like it was bad or lackluster, we will say, "Okay." Rarely do we allow the Holy Spirit to guide our evaluation of the day. Our emotions do the talking.

Have you ever had the feeling that your day was going to be bad? One day, while taking my kids to school, I was struck with this feeling. I began to feel down. Joy leaked out. As I began to settle into a dour outlook, the Holy Spirit reminded me that he wants me to experience joy in all circumstances. He brought Romans 14:17 to mind, "For the kingdom of God is not a matter of eating and drinking but of righteousness and *peace and joy in the Holy Spirit*." Instead of succumbing to my bleak emotions, the Spirit prompted me to believe God's promise and escape the kingdom of despair. I had to choose to trust him, but once I did I entered the joy of the Holy Spirit. The emotional fog lifted, and as I recall, it turned out to be a "pretty good day." I don't remember any confetti or fireworks going off, but I do remember the Spirit's nudge and the power of God's promise being activated in my heart.

I don't want you to get the wrong impression. Emotions certainly aren't bad; it's just that they can be unreliable. For this reason, my old college pastor used to say, "We're made to run on principle not emotion." There are days, and even seasons, when we won't have "all the feels." If we're not careful, we will allow our emotion to cause us to question things we hold dear.

When I meet with couples who are considering divorce, I occasionally hear them say, "We just fell out of love. Does God want us to stay in a loveless marriage?" I respond by asking them, "What do you mean by love?"

In the film *Inception*, the character named Cobb is able to put people into a dream state and then enter their dreams where they can imagine anything. He does this with his wife. In the dream world, they create a charming home, frequent beautiful places, and build an entire city together. It's wonderful *until they have to come back to reality*. Back in the real world, Cobb's wife becomes obsessed with the dream world, blurring the lines between what's real and what's not. She convinces herself that *reality is a dream* and the *dream is reality*. To prove it to her husband, she jumps from an upper story hotel room only to meet her death.

To cope with losing his wife, Cobb puts himself to sleep and goes into his own dreams to visit her in their perfect world. But eventually he has to come to terms with his dream wife. She is not real. She begs him to stay, and he wants to, but he can't. He says: "I wish. I wish more than anything. But I can't imagine you with all your complexity, all your perfection, all your *imperfection*. Look at you. You are just a *shade* of my real wife. You're the best I can do; but I'm sorry, you are just not good enough."

Before he can come to grips with real love, Cobb has to have his vision of love shattered. He has to give up the dream to enter the reality. Before we can truly love one another, we have to give up our dreams of what love looks like. Only then can we enter real love.

One dream of love we must renounce is this: "True love shouldn't be hard." There's a myth out there that says when you find true love, you'll know it because it will be easy. That's how people "fall in love." We approach friends, spouses, even churches this way. So when loving others gets difficult, we conclude we probably need to move on from the relationship. It's hard, so we "fall out of love." But we would never say this about parenting or a job we love. If you love your kids, if you love your work, then it'll never be hard—it will just flow! Not at all. Ask my wife, my kids! Loving me can be hard sometimes, and so can my job. The truth is, love is hard and my wife married a world of imperfections. But isn't this what tipped Cobb off to reality inside his dream world, that his dream wife didn't have the *imperfections* of the real wife? This side of heaven faulty love demands perfection, but real love embraces the imperfections of others and stays the course. It takes a posture of commitment and self-sacrifice.

Returning to the troubled married couple, does God expect them to live in a state of dissatisfaction? Not at all. Again we have to confront our feelings with what is true. Remember what John the Beloved says: "In this is love, not that we have loved God but that he loved us and sent his Son to be the propitiation for our sins" (1 Jn 4:10). God takes the initiative to love us before we possess a drop of love for him. He is the origin and fountain of love. Even non-Christians can identify the difference this makes. A secular couple was describing the challenge of love in their marriage, and the husband said, "One thing I find attractive, that I'm even jealous of in Christianity, is that you have an infinite supply of love to draw from. We combine our finite sources, from friends, our community, our traditions, but that's much harder, and limited. In Christianity, you have an infinite well to draw from." Indeed, the Trinity has invited us into the satisfaction of their undying love. The Father, Son, and Holy Spirit are a whirlwind of love—Lover, Beloved, and Love—extending us never-ending commitment, delight, and affection which frees us to love and serve one another. This is the power of divine love. So the next time you don't feel the love, check your emotions with the promise of God's love. Check your dream with hope of reality.

The final alternative power supply we will consider is *experience*. Perhaps you've heard the millennial mantra, "Spend your money on experiences, not on things." The growing popularity of niche restaurants, music festivals, consumer breweries, in-house coffee roasters, and weekend travel seem to support this mantra. Who doesn't love a great experience, especially when it can live on in Instagram? In the book *The Experience Economy*, Pine and Gillmore insist the best way to a customer's heart is the idea of staging experiences. In Colorado, two breweries transformed a grassy park into a winter playground, bringing in snow to create a three-story ramp to exhibit snowboarding and ski tricks. Commenting on the event, Shannon Berner, Great Divide's marketing manager said, "In craft beer, it's not just about the beer. It's about the community, the lifestyle and the experience." Countless coffee shops brandish community as one of their core values. Cuppings or tastings foster community for the coffee elite. Walking away from a restaurant, we are often prone to comment on our experience even more than the food: "The service was awful," "I loved the ambience," or "The dim sum cart was so cool."

In an experience economy, disciples quickly turn into consumers. Instead of committing ourselves to a life of service, we're disposed to expect the church and the faith to serve us. If the preaching isn't engaging enough, we'll complain, "podcast" another preacher, or just look for another church. I was visiting a church and people from the first service were coming out as my friends and I were going in for the second service. One of my friends asked a first-service person how the message was. He responded by saying, "You'll definitely like the music." The musical experience was prized over the preached Word. Instead, we should prize God over the experience. I wonder how the conversation would have gone if my friend had asked, "What did God say to you in the message?" Perhaps we should ask, "What did God say?" not "How was church?"

In an experience economy we're poised to critique, which places us above the church, not in it. We easily jettison our identity as brothers and sisters within God's family, and service to the community becomes optional or restricted to the elite. But in a healthy family, everyone has a role in the household chores. Just think what could happen in your church if everyone relied on the power of the Holy Spirit to serve rather than be served. Serving wasn't above Jesus: "For even the Son of Man came not to be served but to serve, and to give his life as a ransom for many" (Mk 10:45). Thank God Jesus didn't opt for the best experience.

> In an experience economy we're poised to critique, which places us above the church, not in it.

Experience-driven discipleship can also cause us to get down on ourselves and others. If we don't feel goosebumps in worship when everyone else does, we might start to think of ourselves as spiritually inferior. If we don't grasp a sermon insight the way our friend did, we might berate ourselves for not paying more attention or being theologically sharp. Hearing about a community group that has more of what we're looking for, we may decide to bail on those God has called us to love and serve and switch groups. The secular liturgy of the experience economy wires us for comfort and convenience, but the kingdom of God calls us to take up our cross and deny ourselves.

Contrary to alternative power supplies, the power of the Spirit produces the image of Christ. Like he did with Jesus in the wilderness, the Spirit will prompt us to put faith in God's promises. Therefore, it's important that we regularly pour the promises of God over our hearts so they can be captivated by what is true, good, and beautiful. We should also frequently ask the Holy Spirit to fill us. The more we unplug from reason, emotion, and experience as our power for life and are filled with the Holy Spirit, the more our thinking, feeling, and acting will resemble Jesus. We will grow in confidence of God's love, truth, and grace. Thinking more of Christ and less of ourselves, we will take on an unpretentious humility which leads to spontaneous prayer, service, holiness, and even hope in suffering.

The Shape of Suffering

W HEN I DISCOVERED my aunt's life was in rapid decline due to dual renal failure, I was floored. Although I had known she was facing some medical challenges, I did not realize she had been on dialysis for a year and a half, and that a kidney donation could transform her life. My father told me he had volunteered, but he was not a match. Immediately, I thought to myself, "I am a universal blood donor, O positive." Before I knew it, the same sentence left my lips. That afternoon I discussed the prospect of donating my kidney with my wife. She was immediately supportive. I had no idea what I was getting into.

WHEN YOU AWAKE, I AM WITH YOU

One year later, after tons of testing, pricking, and peeing, I entered the pre-op room. I awoke sluggishly, in a post-op hospital bed, my aunt still in surgery. Although one eye refused to open, I could make out people telling me to eat. I did not want to eat; I wanted unconsciousness, to escape the feeling that I had been run over twice by an eighteen-wheeler. Instead, I began to vomit, over and over again, unable to hold anything down due to a reaction to the anesthesia. The first sign of the Holy Spirit's presence was my wife's swift movement with the barf bucket. She stood there and caught all my stuff. I was able to make out several figures in my room. It was comforting to know that my parents and friends had come to support me.

But when the nights rolled in, and all my supporters were asleep, I was haunted by despair. How long till I can walk properly again? The incisions had severely weakened my abdominal muscles, making it impossible to get out of bed without excruciating pain. Going to the bathroom was an Olympic event and walking felt impossible. Eventually I learned how to shuffle around the nurses' station, with one hand on my IV pole and the other on my wife. But at night I would wonder if I would ever recover. Unable to sleep, the darkness haunted me. Solitude closed in like an enemy. I felt like I was going crazy—until I fumbled my Bible app open to Psalm 139, where I knew I would find comfort in the Spirit's presence:

> Where shall I go from your Spirit?
>   Or where shall I flee from your presence?
> If I ascend to heaven, you are there!
> If I make my bed in Sheol, you are there!
> If I take the wings of the morning
>   and dwell in the uttermost parts of the sea,
> even there your hand shall lead me,
>   and your right hand shall hold me.
> If I say, "Surely the darkness shall cover me,
>   and the light about me be night,"
> even the darkness is not dark to you;

the night is bright as the day,

for darkness is as light with you. (Ps 139:7-12)

I was sweetly assured of the Spirit's presence. If he soars the heights of the heavens and plumbs the depths of the dead, stretches as far east as the rising of the sun, and to the extreme west at the edge of the sea, he can handle a hospital room. The omnidirectional presence of the Spirit leaves not a single crack for us to slip through. No matter how high or how low we get, or how dark or how light our circumstances may be, he is with us. He is not merely present but present with power. The Spirit is so powerful he can burn a hole in the night, which is just what he did for me. Fearful of going to sleep lest I wake up alone in the dark, my eyes fell on this phrase, "I awake, and I am still with you" (Ps 139:18). Me? Yes, you, Jonathan.

> The omnidirectional presence of the Spirit leaves not a single crack for us to slip through.

The light had broken! When everyone else left for their own bed, the Spirit remained. When there is no advocate, the Helper stands up. As I read this promise, I almost cried, but I knew better than to strain my ripped up abdominal muscles. But each time I awoke to pain and despair, I whispered to myself, "When you awake, he is with you." That seven-word promise lifted me out of the doldrums every time. I must have repeated it fifty times in three days.

In the daytime, the Spirit enabled me to lap the nurses' station as often as I could for a quick recovery. I soon found out my aunt's body had received my kidney and that she was in recovery on the same floor. When we suffer and feel alone, we are not. Even there the Spirit's hand will lead us, his right hand will hold us up. The Spirit empowers us in suffering, not simply by helping us to gut it out, but by being faithfully present, going wherever we go, and sturdily leading us toward the light.

HOW JESUS GOT THROUGH SUFFERING

Earlier we saw the Spirit helping Jesus through his time in the wilderness, where he went without food, endured harsh conditions, and was tempted by the devil. As the Suffering Servant, Jesus bore our griefs and our sorrows, was pierced and crushed for our sins, oppressed and afflicted for our peace, and cut off from the land of the living (Is 53:4-8). How did he endure such hostility and pain? Was it because he was superhuman? Actually, Jesus was fully human and fully divine. As a result, he was not immune to the psychological, emotional, and physical toll of his sufferings. Contemplating the agony of the cross in the garden of Gethsemane, Jesus asked the Father if he could avoid the bitter cup of bearing God's wrath on our behalf. Hanging from the cross by nothing but rough iron nails piercing his hands and feet, Jesus cried, "My God, my God, why have you forsaken me?" (Mk 15:34). Hardly immune to the effects of suffering, Jesus bled.

How did he make it through such torment? The writer of Hebrews tells us, "*Through the eternal Spirit* [he] offered himself without blemish to God, [to] purify our conscience from dead works to serve the living God" (Heb 9:14; see also Heb 12:1-2). Why does the author affix the word *eternal* before "Spirit" instead of using the more typical word *holy*? One New Testament scholar comments, "It was the power of the eternal Spirit which enabled Christ to be at the same time both high priest and offering." It's possible the reason the Spirit is called eternal is to emphasize his powerful role in forever holding together Jesus' two natures, human and divine, so that he can be both human sacrifice and divine priest. This means the operative power of the Spirit enabled Jesus not merely to endure suffering but to employ his suffering for our eternal redemption. As a result, Jesus becomes both an example of Spirit dependence *and* the basis of our reception of the Spirit. In light of this magnificent work of the Spirit in and through Jesus, the author of Hebrews goes on to exhort us to hold fast to our hope without wavering in the midst of adversity (Heb 10:23). With the eternal Spirit dwelling in us, we too possess unfathomable resources to suffer for the glory of God.

> With the eternal Spirit dwelling in us, we possess unfathomable resources to suffer for the glory of God.

When we consider Jesus, very often we look to him as an example of godly character, or the basis of forgiveness, but fail to see his example of dependence upon the Spirit. The life of Jesus is exemplary not just in what he did but also how he did it. He was not immune to temptation or impervious to suffering. He fought the good fight of faith, but he did not fight alone. Jesus did not sever himself from the Trinity to accomplish his mission. He remained in communion with the Father and dependent on the Spirit to carry out his work.

Similarly, the Spirit compels us to embrace self-sacrifice for the sake of God's mission, building up the church, spreading the gospel, and renewing the world. In ordinary life, and especially in suffering, we desperately need the continual filling of the Holy Spirit to close the distance on the image of Jesus. Only with him can we show the world the glory of God that is humanity fully alive.

13

Bearing Fruit

ALTHOUGH I'VE TRAINED for a marathon, I've never actually run one. I got pretty darn close, running twenty-two miles when I was training with my girlfriend, but then we broke up. I know—it's not the same as running a full marathon. She told me all about it.

It all begins with the starting-line warmup. Innumerable bodies collect, like hundreds of ball bearings to a magnet. Annoying rock music blares in the background, and human limbs begin to stretch, bibs get repinned, and heartrates increase. Sweatshirts and warmup suits are thrown to bleary-eyed supporters as the countdown commences. Your mind drifts to how hard you've trained to get here—you can do this!—and you're suddenly gripped by the dream that got you here, why you're doing this. Enraptured by visions of crossing the finish line, extremities tingle with excitement; the pistol is fired and the pack lurches forward.

The first five miles are flat out fun. Friends and family members line the course with homemade posters calling out in enthusiastic support as their loved ones jog by. Runners reluctantly dart in and out of porta potties as the pack separates like goo, congealing in blobs determined by pace. Further in, you hit your stride and begin to take in the beauty of it all. You pass smiley, power-of-positive-thinking volunteers who extend plastic cups of water. About halfway in the endorphins have settled down and your thoughts begin to climb for motivation. Water stations and power gels start to look appealing. You veer over for a boost and keep running.

Then about three quarters of the way into the race, you suddenly become aware of every discomfort and potential injury. Running begins to feel like plodding. Your head throbs and your throat feels dry. The blob has disintegrated, creating a sense of isolation. The excitement fades as running a marathon devolves into a mundane, even boring, activity. Why did I do this? Is it worth it? Will I make it to the finish line? Your thoughts drift to more satisfying things, like eating whatever fattening food you can dream of and chasing it with an ice-cold drink. Fatigue sets in and you smell the salt on your body. Your quads and calves agonize with each stride. Encouragement has thinned out from the sidelines and you think about quitting.

FINISHING IN THE SPIRIT

In many ways, running a marathon is like the Christian life. We start off with an explosion of joy, surrounded by others and enamored with the risen Christ. The Bible is fresh, each story and chapter electrified by the Holy Spirit. Sunday worship is always awesome and holiness matters as much as getting plugged in. But eventually, the prongs loosen from the socket. The difficulty of following Jesus sets in and suddenly Christianity begins to lose its luster. You daydream about spending less time with Jesus and the church, and the dream becomes a reality. Other things begin to captivate your imagination. Christians begin to look like water station groupies, smiles plastered across their faces, and there are stretches where you feel like you're just putting one foot in front of the other. You had no idea the faith could be so boring.

It is perhaps here, in the ordinariness of life, that we need the Holy Spirit most. St. Paul puts it to us like this, "Are you so foolish? Having begun by the Spirit, are you now being perfected by the flesh?" (Gal 3:3). It's so easy to drift from life in the Spirit. Before we know it, our jog has slowed to a crawl. But it is here, in the grittiness and tedium of life, where our discipleship is worked out and a vision for holiness is needed.

ORDINARY SPIRIT

Two things await us when we wake—God and our smartphone. One Monday morning I woke up, turned off the alarm on my phone, and against my better judgment, checked my email. There was a message from a young lady who was spinning away from Christ and struggling with depression. She was announcing her departure from our church. The email sent my mind reeling. I'd spent quite a bit of time with her, and my heart ached for her.

I climbed out of bed and made my way to the shower, where a host of questions hit me all at once. How should I respond? Should I email or call? Would pressing for one last meeting be worth it? What would I say? How can I help her discover the source of her depression, so she can climb out of it, and fight for joy with the help of other struggling saints? When I sat down to commune with God, I couldn't get my mind to switch over. I wanted to "taste and see the Lord is good," but I had become hungrier for something else—resolution.

Both our responsibilities and our Lord beckon us in the morning. Jesus says, "Come to me, all who labor and are heavy laden, and I will give you rest" (Mt 11:28). Even after a good night's sleep, we awake in need of rest. Rest from what? Rest from the looming anxieties of the day that peer down the tower of our responsibility. Spiritual rest.

Dallas Willard was asked to describe Jesus in one word. What word would you pick? Merciful? Kind? Powerful? Do you know what Willard said? *Relaxed.* I wouldn't have said that in a million years, but if you think about it, Jesus never moved through life in a hurry. He even deliberately delayed responsibilities to attend to other people. Jesus wasn't dominated by the cares of the world, despite the fact that the world was on his shoulders. How did he do it? He prayed. Not the dutiful, make-your-way-through-the-list kind of praying, but communion-with-the-Father kind of praying: "And rising very early in the morning, while it was still dark, he departed and went out to a desolate place, and there he prayed" (Mk 1:35). We know this was a regular occurrence for Jesus because Luke says, "But he would withdraw to desolate places and pray" (Lk 5:16). The *but* in this sentence is there to mark a contrast with all of Jesus' impending responsibilities—the crowds who gathered to hear him and the sick who longed to be healed. And in the face of those good obligations, Jesus left. Walked away. Before anyone would notice, he stole away to a quiet place to be with his heavenly Father.

For years I've begun my day by praying the Lord's Prayer, pausing to personalize each phrase. "Our Father who art in heaven, hallowed be your name." Then I ask him to help me hallow or glorify him in my various roles: "Lord, help me to glorify you as a loving husband, tender father, wise pastor, and creative, truth-telling author." Then I would move onto the next bit, until one day the Lord stopped me: "Jonathan, you've been skipping over the best part of my prayer, 'Our Father.' Don't you know that's how I want you to start your day? Not with your roles and responsibilities, but with your identity as my free and loved son?" Mic drop. Tears flowed. He's really that good, and I forget it all the time, even in prayer. James says, "He yearns jealously over the spirit that he has made to dwell in us" (Jas 4:5). God isn't a passive, disinterested father; he's a burning-with-holy-jealous-love kind of father. All too often I make him out to be something else, even though I *know* he isn't.

One day I was backing my dad's new sports car out of the garage and scraped up one of the wheels. I felt awful and told myself off, "You're an idiot." Since my dad was away, I took a picture of the wheel and planned to send it to him. It took me a couple days to actually send it. I wondered how mad he would be. I'd offer to pay for it—but how much do those things cost? I finally braved the text and waited and waited and waited. Hours later, I followed up with another text, "Hope the silence isn't your disappointment."

He replied, "Just got this. Things happen. Don't worry about it."

What?! That easy? Then I thought to myself, *Has your dad ever flown off the handle when you've busted something?* No. He's not like that; he loves me. Suddenly I realized I had been looking at my dad through my responsibility, my mistake, not through his incredible love for me. Then the Spirit showed me this is how I sometimes view my heavenly Father, expecting him to fly off the handle when his arms are actually wide open. When we're driven by tasks and responsibilities, whether we've failed or succeeded, it's easy to lose sight of how much the Father loves us.

> This is how I sometimes view my heavenly Father, expecting him to fly off the handle when his arms are actually wide open.

The Father earnestly desires his spirit *in you*. Why the "spirit"? Not because he doesn't love *you*, but because he loves the new you, the one indwelt by his very own Spirit who cries out "Abba! Father!" (Gal 4:6). He doesn't relate to you on the basis of the old you. His Son died for that. He relates to the new you, the true you. The Father is head over heels in love with you, and the Spirit is there, every morning, silently reminding us of the Father's love, before we climb a single step of responsibility. Contrary to the message, "You are what you do," he says, "You are who I made you—my child fully loved and fully accepted." Now I begin my day by praying, "Our Father who art in heaven; thank you for letting me enjoy your favor as a son before I do a single thing today." Game changer.

Beginning with our first breath, the Spirit wants to get into the nitty-gritty of our day. He's the one who prompts us, the moment we wake, to turn to the Father, and he's there prompting us throughout the day. Richard Lovelace recommends,

> We should make a deliberate effort at the outset of every day to recognize the person of the Holy Spirit, to move into the light concerning his presence in our consciousness and to open up our minds and to share all our thoughts and plans as we gaze by faith into the face of God. We should continue to walk throughout the day in a relationship of communication and communion with the Spirit mediated through our knowledge of the Word, relying upon every office of the Holy Spirit's role as counselor mentioned in Scripture.

Very often the Spirit is the voice in our head nudging us to serve others. Some days I'll be at work, head down, and I'll think, "I should buy Robie flowers on the way home." Sometimes I'll respond by thinking back, "That's a great idea, but I'm too busy to think about that now," or "I'll try to remember when I leave from work." But if I'm attuned to the Spirit, I will recognize his voice working through my natural affection for my wife and make a mental note to buy flowers on the way home. She hasn't turned them down yet.

The Spirit—not our noble, inner self—is the prod to serve others. The Spirit may spark ideas like cleaning the house or giving our spouse a night out, babysitting for a couple, asking a single over for dinner, or blessing someone with an act of unexpected financial generosity. Or perhaps the Spirit will prod you to serve your church somehow, like caring for the little kids, helping with menial tasks, or stepping up to lead a community group or ministry. The Spirit is always intent on making us into the likeness of Jesus, who came "not to be served but to serve, and to give his life as a ransom for many" (Mk 10:45). Don't write the Spirit's voice off as a moment of personal inspiration. Listen, lean in, and act.

> The Spirit—not our noble, inner self— is the prod to serve others.

PRAYING ON THE SPOT

Another way the Spirit works in the ordinary is by "putting people on our hearts." Have you ever had someone tell you they were thinking of you earlier in the week and paused to pray for you? It's a real blessing to know that God loves you enough to put you on someone else's heart. Paul tells us that we are to pray "in the Spirit" at all times, with all prayer and supplication (Eph 6:18). Supplication is an old word that means to humbly request, but the Greek word fills the request with urgency, meaning "an urgent request to meet a need." When we are walking in the Spirit, he will occasionally bring names to mind so we can pray for them.

A guy in our church was struggling with discouragement, and after praying with his wife for joy, he received a text from a friend that said, "I'm praying for increased joy in the Lord." Sometimes it's that simple, but profound. He shared with me just how moving it was to know the Lord was so attentive to his prayer. A number of people in our church have taken up texting one another words of encouragement throughout the day. Sometimes this is the result of planned Bible study together, and other times it's spontaneous. Either way, the Spirit often connects them in a moment of need. Remember Psalm 139—the Spirit is everywhere and with everyone at once. He knows all things and loves to connect our prayers with others' needs. Sometimes this happens on the spot.

Have you ever opened up to share a personal need or struggle with someone, and in response they say, "I'll pray for you"? Prayer is one of the most loving things we can do for someone. This is because prayer is taking people's greatest needs to the wisest, most powerful being in the universe. The Lord's arm is not too short to save (Is 59:1), and his arsenal is the city of Zion. The reverse is true too—neglect of prayer is a serious lapse of love. Have you ever promised to pray for someone, but failed to follow through? Or in a moment of your own need, have you walked away from a conversation wishing your friend would have prayed for you right there and then? I know someone who, after listening intently to people, responds by offering to pray for them on the spot. What would happen if we all did that? Not in a creepy, cultic, lockstep way, but whenever we sense it's good timing, when prompted by the Spirit. That would be a force to reckon with. It raises the question: If we are supposed to pray at all times in the Spirit in urgent intercession for others, why don't we do it?

I read an article years ago that suggested the "mediatorial elite" is a barrier to spontaneous prayer. I vaguely recall it describing a social dynamic among Christians where people don't pray out loud because we perceive our prayers to be inferior to the spiritual giants in the room. The author debunked this idea by pointing to the priestly work of Christ, who has passed through the heavens making it possible for *all* to draw near to the throne of God with confidence to receive grace to help in time of need (Heb 4:14-16).

In order to be bolder in prayer, to act in love and take the needs of others to God, we may need to confront the false notion of a "mediatorial elite." This might begin by repenting of being overly concerned with what others think of our praying, asking Jesus to forgive us for minimizing *his* mediatorial work on our behalf. There is no mediatorial elite. Then we can exercise greater faith in Jesus as we pray for others. We are a kingdom of priests, living stones that compose a holy, cosmic temple where the Spirit dwells, prompting urgent prayers for the people and mission of God. So let's get on with praying out loud, on the spot, in intercession for others.

I was walking with a friend through the streets of a village in northern Thailand. Surrounded by opulent Buddhist temples covered in gold flake, we were cut to the heart by the spiritual poverty all around us. As we lamented the beautiful deception, my friend piped up and said, "Let's throw up the true temple and pray for this place." As we prayed and called on the name of the Lord, the Spirit's presence throbbed in the midst of this remote Buddhist village. Who knows what the Lord did in answer to those prayers? Just think what could happen in our own villages if we "threw up the true temple" more often and prayed for others in the moment.

THE SHAPE OF FRUIT

In addition to praying, how else can we heed Paul's exhortation to walk in the Spirit? He writes, "But I say, walk by the Spirit, and you will not gratify the desires of the flesh" (Gal 5:16). While it's likely Paul chose this metaphor with walking with God in view, it is equally likely he selected it for its ordinary value. Walking is something we do almost entirely unconsciously. Think about it—when is the last time you focused on how to walk? Probably when you were doing something out of the ordinary, like hiking. Paul wants us to pick up on the fact that the Spirit is for everyone in everyday life, not just on special excursions. His primary reason for this emphasis here is to combat the everyday alternative—walking in the flesh.

Richard Lovelace describes the flesh as "the fallen human personality apart from the renewing influence and control of the Holy Spirit." Apart from the Spirit, we devolve into a fallen version of ourselves, ruled by things like vanity, sloth, lust, anger, jealousy, and pride. With the Spirit, however, we bear the fruit of "love, joy, peace, patience, kindness, goodness, faithfulness, gentleness, self-control" (Gal 5:22-23). Commenting on this verse, Mark Sayers notes, "This fruit cannot be bought, or downloaded; instead it emerges from an inner life, shaped by the reality of fighting the flesh, of living by the Spirit in the church."

Bearing the fruit of the Spirit is a *community* endeavor. We cannot love if we do not put ourselves in the service of those we find difficult to love. We cannot be kind to ourselves; kindness is for those around us. We can pray for patience all day, but seeing it modeled in others is a tremendous help. Joy is incomplete until it's expressed; in fact, it increases when we invite others to share in it. Joy bubbles up in fellowship, overflows in evangelism, and compounds in corporate worship. The fruit of the Spirit has a distinctly communal shape. It isn't just for us; it's for the world.

> Joy is incomplete until it's expressed.

But as Sayers points out, the fruit doesn't come easily. Looking at these lists, sometimes we feel more in touch with the vices than the virtues. The Spirit and the flesh dichotomy can be maddening: "For the desires of the flesh are against the Spirit, and the desires of the Spirit are against the flesh, for these are opposed to each other, to keep you from doing the things you want to do" (Gal 5:17). Like in *The Strange Case of Dr. Jekyll and Mr. Hyde*, we often find ourselves ingratiating our bad side when we really want to live out our good side. Jekyll reflects:

> If each, I told myself, could but be housed in separate identities, life would be relieved of all that was unbearable; the unjust delivered from the aspirations might go his way, and remorse of his more upright twin; and the just could walk steadfastly and securely on his upward path, doing the good things in which he found his pleasure, and no longer exposed to disgrace and penitence by the hands of this extraneous evil.

Perceiving two distinct natures within himself, Jekyll finds hope in separating the two identities. But Paul goes in a different direction: "I have been crucified with Christ. It is no longer I who live, but Christ who lives in me" (Gal 2:20). In Christ, the old identity is crucified, not separated, so the new identity can live on. This single, secure identity gives us the upper hand in fighting fleshly evils. In fact, after voicing his bitter battle—"for I do not do the good I want, but the evil I do not want is what I keep on doing" (Rom 7:19)—Paul reminds us that the Spirit has swung the cage door open to liberate us from the prison of the flesh: "*For the law of the Spirit of life has set you free* in Christ Jesus from the law of sin and death" (Rom 8:2). We are no longer slaves to sin but sons of God. The Spirit sprang us from the flesh so we can run into the arms of the Father. He says, "Go, run! You're free."

> The Spirit has swung the cage door open to liberate us from the prison of the flesh.

A HABITUAL VISION OF GREATNESS

When soldiers come home from war they are often plagued by a haunting question, "Was it worth it?" When we stand before the Lord of history, we will not regret a single drop of effort spent fighting for the fruit of the Spirit. Paul writes, "For if you live according to the flesh you will die, but if by the Spirit you put to death the deeds of the body, you will live" (Rom 8:13). The New Testament frequently exhorts us to mortify the flesh (Eph 4:22-23; Col 3:5-6; Heb 3:12-13). *Mortify* is an old word meaning "to put to death," and its use here implies a tenacious disposition of the heart that longs to defeat sin out of love for Jesus.

Sometimes we lose sight of Jesus as the ultimate goal of our fight. Overcome by our failures or enthralled by temptations, we are blinded to the glory and beauty of Christ. But Paul keeps the ultimate goal in view—*that you will live*. The promise of eternal life can feel so distant that it's hard to feel motivated to fight the flesh in everyday life. But eternal life isn't merely the promise of long life in heaven; it is life with Jesus now. Jesus himself said, "And this is eternal life, that they know you, the only true God, and Jesus Christ, whom you have sent" (Jn 17:3). David Ford comments, "One of John's favorite phrases, 'eternal life' is not so much about 'life after death' as 'life after the death and resurrection of Jesus'—life, with others, abiding in him, loved by him, and loving him." Our struggle, then, is not merely to put the flesh to death but to enjoy life with God in Christ! Jesus is the great reward of the soul who makes all our bruises and wounds worth it.

When I write I like to get away to remote places. This is partly due to the silence and space for reflection they afford, but it's also because I like to be surrounded by natural beauty. When I hit a rough patch or run headlong into writer's block, I can walk out my door, lift my eyes, and soak in the greatness around me. This gives my left brain a break so my right brain can kick in with creative inspiration, but more importantly it redirects my attention to the reason I'm writing at all—to apprehend and convey the beauty I see in front of me. Similarly, we need what Alfred North Whitehead called "a habitual vision of greatness." We need something epic to love if we are to walk faithfully with the Spirit and bear his fruit in this world. Christ is that vision of greatness: "He is the image of the invisible God, the firstborn of all creation" (Col 1:15), "the Lamb of God who takes away the sins of the world" (Jn 1:29), the Son of Man whose face shines like the sun and whose eyes are an ocean of love. He is the magistrate who will judge the quick and the dead, and the One who will make all things new. The Lord Jesus Christ is our habitual vision of greatness, and the Spirit gives us the ability to take him in. We mortify the flesh by the Spirit to take in Jesus. That little prepositional phrase "by the Spirit" is important. By the Spirit Jesus cast out demons (Mt 12:28) and

contended with the devil (Mt 4:1), and by the same Spirit we bear
the fruit of his character. Bearing fruit isn't something we do on
our own. The power the Spirit gives us, over even the most difficult
of temptations, flows freely through his Word and his people.

FRUITFUL TOGETHER

If it weren't for friends who fight for my sanctification, I would
have made an utter wreck of my faith by now. Over the years, these
friends have exhorted me to treasure Jesus, called me to repentance
over sin, held me accountable in avoiding certain temptations, and
reveled with me in the gospel of the glory of God. You don't just
happen into these kinds of friendships. You have to seek them out
and work on them.

Every other Friday I meet a friend for coffee to discuss what
we're reading in Scripture and how the Holy Spirit is speaking to
us through it. We try not to focus on current events, though those
can be quite relevant to our discipleship, but hone in on holiness
together. We try to listen well, exhort and encourage one another
in the Scriptures, and pray on the spot. When we need it, we
extend sympathy to one another through seasons of hardship and
pain. We pray for our spouses and children, and for our church.
It's not flashy, but there's power in it, the power of the extraordinary
Spirit flowing through fellowship in ordinary life. That meeting is
sticky. What happens there stretches out into the week, touching
our thoughts and actions, pulling them in a Christward direction.
This results in occasional texts of encouragement, regular prayer for
one another, and a thickness to our friendship outside of our meeting.
We do ordinary stuff together too, like watch movies and just hang
out. Sometimes I daydream of sharing a personal joy with him

when he's not around. Godly friends haunt us like specters of love, truth, and grace that call us into Christlikeness.

Men in particular often fail to make time for these relationships. As a result they often stumble in isolation, but as we've seen, our sin refuses to remain isolated. The fruit of the Spirit is cultivated in community, and our freedom is meant to be for one another: "For you were called to freedom, brothers. Only do not use your freedom as an opportunity for the flesh, *but through love serve one another*" (Gal 5:13). We yield to the Spirit's prompts to bear fruit together.

I STILL HAVEN'T FOUND WHAT I'M LOOKING FOR

I missed my first U2 concert when I was a junior in high school. A friend offered to get tickets to the Zoo TV Tour, but for some reason it didn't work out. I wish I could have seen those German cars on stilts and heard Bono croon "Even Better Than the Real Thing." But missing that show didn't keep me from total fandom. In the years to come I bought every CD, including bootlegs, snapped up as much literature on the band as I could, watched *Rattle & Hum*, and prayed for Bono during his MacPhisto days. I shared this love of U2 with my best friend Chris Allred. We'd turn up *Achtung Baby* full blast in his Honda Accord, windows down, while cruising around Deep Ellum. And when the next tour came around, we got tickets to our first U2 concert.

Months before the concert, Chris committed suicide. When I went to see his parents, they directed me to their bedroom and handed me an envelope that said "JD" on it. In it was a letter of apology and our two U2 tickets. I would be going without him. We'd always loved U2's *Joshua Tree* album, but had debated the meaning of the song "I Still Haven't Found What I'm Looking

For." As Christians, we had a hard time reconciling Jesus breaking our bonds with the song's apparent insistence that there was still something missing: "You broke the bonds, And you loosed the chains, Carried the cross of my shame," together with "But I still haven't found what I'm looking for." How could Bono—and now Chris—sense the freedom of Christ's cross so deeply *and* yet cry out, "I still haven't found what I'm looking for"? Hadn't they, like me, found what they were looking for in Jesus?

Years later, it hit me while driving through the rolling green hills of Ireland—*I* still haven't found what *I'm* looking for. The beauty of this world, and the matchless grace of the cross, exist in a world marred by suicide and sin. No, this is not all I am waiting for. The cross comes before the new creation. Jesus is bringing so much more, more than my twentysomething self could have known to long for, but something my fortysomething self is now in touch with—the Spirit-perfected future of God's new world.

The Future of the Spirit

IN THE FUTURE depicted in Ray Bradbury's *Fahrenheit 451*, firefighters start fires rather than stopping them. They burn books, and houses that contain books, for pleasure. Montag, the fireman, reflects:

> It was a special pleasure to see things eaten, to see things blackened and changed. With the brass nozzle in his fists, with this great python spitting its venomous kerosene upon the world, the blood pounded in his head, and his hands were the hands of some amazing conductor playing all the symphonies of blazing and burning to bring down the tatters and charcoal ruins of history . . . while the flapping pigeon-winged books died on the porch and lawn of the house.

In Montag's world, the reading of books is no longer permitted. If someone is caught with books on philosophy, sociology, or religion, they face extra penalties for crimes against the state. Data is in, but literature is out.

But literature isn't the only thing in decline. The world had endured two atomic wars with devastating effects. In addition, people no longer know how to have meaningful conversation. Everything is superficial: "An hour of TV class, an hour of basketball or baseball or running ... but do you know, we never ask questions, or at least most don't; they just run the answers at you bing, bing, bing, and us sitting there." People just talk *at* one another, humankind reduced to corpses of entertainment, the world virtually void of truth, beauty, and goodness. *Fahrenheit 451* depicts a future where the world is physically, culturally, and humanly broken. With these realities trending *now* in our own culture, are we destined for the same dismal future?

TWO FUTURES

When thinking about the future, two possibilities are typically predicted—utopia or dystopia, heaven or hell. The book *Heaven Is for Real* takes the utopian route, detailing a firsthand account of heaven from the near-death experience of a three-year-old. Apparently, his glimpses of the future include Jesus riding on a rainbow horse and angels serenading the saints. In addition to being boring and publicly disavowed, this description of heaven is theologically topsy-turvy. When angels sing in Scripture, it is always out of adoration of the holy Trinity, not to comfort or entertain us (Is 6:1-3; Lk 2:14; Rev 4:1-8). Moreover, it's better to get our notions of heaven from the Bible than from a child or an adult who claims to have spent ninety minutes in heaven.

Alternatively, popular culture continues to churn out dystopian visions of the future where hope is all but dried up and peace is nowhere to be found, such as the bleak landscape of *Mad Max* and the zombie-filled *The Walking Dead*. But these dystopias do get you thinking. Is an apocalypse like this on its way? Which future should we anticipate?

THE END OF THE WORLD

The "end" of the world is described in various places throughout Scripture. Peter, a disciple of Jesus and leader of the church in Jerusalem, describes the future of the world in terms of a coming day of judgment, when "the heavens will pass away with a roar, and the heavenly bodies will be burned up and dissolved, and the earth and the works that are done on it will be exposed" (2 Pet 3:10). According to this verse, three layers of the cosmos will be affected: the heavens, the heavenly bodies, and the earth itself.

First, we're told when the Day of the Lord comes, the *heavens* will pass away with a roar. The word *roar* refers to a rushing sound, which is sometimes compared to the whiz of an arrow or the rush of wings. Although this is the only occurrence of this word in the Bible, it does call to mind the wind and bird images of the Spirit. Employing a similar idea, the prophet Isaiah describes a day when the heavens will be rolled up like a scroll (Is 34:4). Although we cannot be certain, it is possible these images depict the Spirit's role in judging the world through an act of de-creation. With the celestial boundary removed, the cosmos would be exposed, and the earth in particular, to the visible powers and authorities of heaven, including Christ and his angels. With the metaphysical barrier between us and God gone, we will be placed in the precarious position of witnessing the judgment and salvation of God.

Next, we're told the "heavenly bodies" will be burned up and dissolved. The meaning of this word is debated among scholars, ranging from "stars" to the "primal elements" of the universe. Regardless of the meaning, this second layer seems to deal with actual cosmic bodies rather than a celestial barrier. We can envision easy parallels with the implosion of the sun or the shrinking of dark energy resulting in what theoretical physicists call the Big Crunch. Whatever the case, stars or elements will be dissolved by fire.

Finally, the earth and the works that are done on the earth will be exposed. If the elements of the universe are burning, it stands to follow that there will be some kind of conflagration on earth. One can envision the stripping away of the heavens and the stars, and the earth laid bare exposed before the cosmic judge. While we cannot be too rigid in predicting what will happen, it is clear that somehow God will judge and purify the cosmos. The day of reckoning is coming and the Spirit will be involved. Therefore, it is unwise to live as though we can fashion meaning, employ creativity, and seek satisfaction wherever we wish. Rather, we should keep in step with the Spirit and look to Christ for these things. As an old Puritan once wrote, God threatens terrible things if we will not be happy.

The good news is that the Lord has tarried, and he wills that none should perish but that all should reach repentance (2 Pet 3:9). The kingdom of God is slowly breaking into this world, and that is to our advantage, that more might clutch the offer of the crucified Christ. Forgiveness and deliverance are possible because Jesus endured the early apocalypse of God's wrath for our sin at his cross.

THE RENEWAL OF THE WORLD

The alternate, utopian ending also includes the work of the Holy Spirit. In the book of Revelation, the Spirit appears eighteen times. He first appears in a trinitarian greeting from the book's author, John: "Grace to you and peace from him who is and who was and who is to come, and from the seven spirits who are before his throne" (Rev 1:4; cf. Rev 3:1; 4:5; 5:6). The "seven spirits before the throne" are a symbolic image of the Spirit. Why seven spirits? The number seven is also used to refer to the Spirit anointing the Messiah in sevenfold wisdom in Isaiah 11:2. The numerical symbol is used to communicate the Spirit's complete wisdom and perfecting ability, a symbol quite appropriate as John considers the work of the Spirit in bringing God's creation project to a climax.

The place of the Spirit "before the throne" reminds us the Spirit is both present and future. He dwells in the elect of God while also dwelling in the very presence of God. Sharing God's attribute of omnipresence, the Spirit is present in heaven and on earth. As this "forever" Spirit (Jn 14:16), he is uniquely positioned to chart a glorious future. While his dissolution of creation is sobering, it is intended to point us to the glory of God, a glory vividly displayed by the Holy Spirit when he also renews the earth. Yes, it is not all doom and gloom.

The Spirit will consummate his creation project in a massive renewal of all things. The alternate ending is a new heavens and a new earth in which righteousness dwells (2 Pet 3:13). But how do we reconcile the elements burning with intense heat with a renewed heavens and earth? In his commentary on 2 Peter 3:10, John Calvin says, "Of the elements of the world I shall only say this one thing, that they are to be consumed, only that they may be renovated, their substance still remaining the same." Somehow God will purify the elements of the earth to reuse them in his renewal of all creation. He does not discard his creation; he remakes it into a place where righteousness dwells. This means justice will move, not just into the neighborhood, but into all of space and time, securing a renewed cosmos populated by transformed people in a world of unimpeachable, never-ending goodness.

> Somehow God will purify the elements of the earth to reuse them in his renewal of all creation.

But what will happen to God's people during the cosmic con-flagration? The Spirit will protect them. During the exodus, the Spirit-cloud moved from in front of Israel to behind them to protect them from the armies of Egypt as they crossed the Red Sea (Ex 14:19-20). Similarly, the Spirit will hover over the people of God again to protect them with a *canopy of glory*: "Then the LORD will create over the whole site of Mount Zion and over her assemblies a cloud by day, and smoke and the shining of a flaming fire by night; for over all the glory there will be a canopy. There will be a booth for shade by day from the heat, and for a refuge and a shelter from the storm and rain" (Is 4:5-6). Although we can't be sure on the specifics, the Spirit will create some kind of enclave for God's people amidst the dissolution and renewal of all things. In the future, the Spirit will sustain and perfect just as he has done all along.

The Spirit's perfecting work will not be restricted to the cosmos but will extend to our very own bodies. In his mesmerizing chapter on the resurrection, Paul describes our bodily transformation, noting that the natural body will become a spiritual body. Like the resur-rected Christ, our physical bodies will be suffused with the Spirit's transformative presence. In fact, the Spirit-enabled resurrection of Jesus becomes the power source for a whole new humanity, "If there is a natural body, there is also a spiritual body. Thus it is written: 'The first man Adam became a living being'; the last Adam became a life-giving spirit" (1 Cor 15:44-45). Christ's resurrection body, a prototype for all Christians, is described in Greek as *pneumatikos*, a body that generates life because of the Spirit within it. Because Christ's work defeated sin, death, and hell, we will live forever in an embodied, glorified state rendered possible by the Spirit's rehabilitative presence. As a result, we will "bear the image of the man of heaven" (1 Cor 15:49).

WILL HEAVEN BE BORING?

With the contours of creation's future in place, we're left to ponder what we will do in heaven. Will it be boring? Through his Spirit-filled prophecy, John records a vision of the new heavens and earth that includes three primary images: a new creation, a bride, and a city (Rev 21). These three images outline the basic features of heavenly existence. As we have already seen, the presence of a new creation reveals that heaven will be a physical place, a renovated form of the present world. The bride imagery reminds us that God will dwell forever with his resplendent people in perfect love and community. The vision of the new Jerusalem tells us that the future will be partially urban, filled with the culture and creative activity associated with city life.

How can we be sure there will be cultural activity in the new creation? Recalling humanity's original purpose from Genesis 1, we saw that the Spirit gave humanity life to rule and relate in his world. This purpose was uniquely embedded in humanity, the only creatures to bear the image of God. Therefore, it would be contrary to our humanity to abandon this purpose in heaven. Rather than lose this ability, our upgraded existence will only enhance our ability as subcreators. We should expect unprecedented works of culture through our perfect cooperation with the Spirit in the future. To get an idea of what we'll be doing, let's take a look inside the new Jerusalem.

FUTURE CULTURE

Inside the new Jerusalem the kings and nations of the earth bring their glory and honor: "By its light will the nations walk, and the kings of the earth will bring their glory into it, and its gates will never be shut by day—and there will be no night there. They will bring into it the glory and the honor of the nations" (Rev 21:24-26). What is this "glory and honor"? Perhaps we are meant to view this as a nonstop worship service—a procession of singing kings that successively bow down before God and then go back to the end of the line only to repeat the process? This would certainly be an act of worship. But what kind of songs—sixth-century Gregorian chants, eighteenth-century English hymns, twentieth-century rock? And in what language will they sing—Japanese, Swahili, Urdu, Tamil, English? What instruments will be used? Will the songs be accompanied by art, poetry, spoken word? This just scratches the surface of cultural activity in the city.

How we interpret these two words—*glory* and *honor*—has significant implications for our understanding of heavenly activity. The words are used together in Exodus 28:2 to refer to the elaborately woven robes worn by the high priest, expanding the possible range of meaning to include physical things like clothing. However, the best way to make sense of these words, and the text as a whole, is to go to John's inspirational source, Isaiah 60.

Throughout Revelation 21–22, John relies heavily on the vision in Isaiah 60, where the nations and kings stream into Zion, the city of God. John's vision of "heaven" is constructed on Isaiah's vision of the future earth. The chapters are complementary. In Isaiah, the people bring the "wealth of the nations" (Is 60:5) into the city as an act of tribute. Consider the list: sheep, camels, gold, frankincense, silver, iron, cypress, and pine. The wealth of the nations is the best produce of the nations, cultural products created by people and dedicated to God. These items require cultural activity. Camels and sheep have to be herded and fed. Gold, silver, and iron have to be mined and put through metallurgical purification, which entails leaching and smelting. Frankincense has to be obtained from the resin in Boswellia trees and then converted into perfume. The industries necessary to develop these things (with eco-friendly energy, no doubt) will enable ongoing cultural activity.

FUTURE LEARNING

As the most creative being in the universe, the Spirit will continue to compel creativity in the new creation. What will we do with the culture we make? No doubt we will enjoy it, but we will also reflect on it. If culture is what we make of the world, it follows that both *making* and *learning* about what we make can honor God. As the Spirit inspired Israel to learn (Neh 9:20) and guides the church into "all truth" (Jn 16:13), he will continue to spark intellectual activity as we innovate, theologize, and learn. It is not as though, in reaching the new creation, we will summit our comprehension of God. In fact, any God that can be fully comprehended is an idol. Idols can be mastered but not the one, true God. Rather, we will continually explore the inexhaustible riches of Christ and ponder the complexity, beauty, and goodness of the unsearchable God (Job 5:9; Is 40:28; Rom 11:33; Eph 3:8). No doubt new scientific theories will be made, architectural feats accomplished, and entirely new disciplines of thought will emerge fostering wonder and awe over the triune God. The eternal Spirit will continue to instruct us in the age to come as we cooperate with him to make and reflect on culture forever in the city of God.

We will continually explore the inexhaustible riches of Christ and ponder the complexity, beauty, and goodness of the unsearchable God.

Moreover, the cultural products we produce will be high grade. Isaiah says:

> All the flocks of Kedar shall be gathered to you;
>> the rams of Nebaioth shall minister to you;
> they shall come up with acceptance on my altar,
>> and I will beautify my beautiful house. (Is 60:7)

Notice these are not shoddy cultural products. The nations do not bring pulpboard; they bring cypress wood. They bring gold, not aluminum. Whatever your cup of tea, from coding to painting, your work will produce results better than your wildest dreams! We will fashion new technologies, explore new worlds, and happen on new insights. We cannot out-dream or out-imagine God. The glory and honor brought before God and the Lamb is physical-cultural tribute.

Why will we do all this? Isaiah gives us two reasons. The *penultimate* reason is to adorn the city, to "beautify" his "beautiful house." The Lord is worthy of excellent, diverse, cultural praise, which will be represented by the various ethnic peoples of the world, and perhaps even by the cultural accomplishments of the past. It is possible, for instance, that the Eiffel Tower, Machu Picchu, the Sistine Chapel, the Great Pyramid of Giza, Beethoven's eighth symphony, and Monet's *Water Lilies* will survive the reconstitution of creation. Of course, any hint of evil will be removed as "nothing unclean will ever enter it" (Rev 21:27).

The *ultimate* reason we will continue to make culture will be to bring praise to God. The nations bring their cultural treasures as "gifts of praise" to the Lord. Making great culture glorifies God when it is done not to magnify our gifts, but to express praise to the Creator. Creative, artistic expression exists to edify others and honor the Creator. Our future is a city teeming with creativity for the glory of God.

> Our future is a city teeming with creativity for the glory of God.

A BEAUTIFUL BRIDE

No one wakes up in the morning, looks into the mirror while brushing their teeth, and thinks, "If only I had a few more wrinkles and a tad more fat." Instead we think, "If I could lose a few wrinkles, maybe even a few pounds, perhaps move up the ladder . . ." Deep down, in some way, we all want to be more beautiful. Revelation 21–22 shows us we need beauty more than we even comprehend.

While suffering in imprisonment on the island of Crete, John receives a vision of great beauty for the persecuted saints: "Come, I will show you the Bride, the wife of the Lamb" (Rev 21:9). The bride is alternatively described as a holy city "coming down out of heaven from God, having the glory of God, its radiance like a most rare jewel, like a jasper, clear as crystal" (Rev 21:10-11). The beauty of the city is compared to a rare jewel and described as "pure gold, like clear glass" (Rev 21:18). This is a picture of *you*, a resplendent city, covered in brilliant jewels, gleaming with gold that's like glass. It can be difficult to picture such beauty.

The closest thing I've seen to a "pure gold" city is the temple compound of the Emerald Buddha in Bangkok, Thailand. Since most of us haven't seen these temples, perhaps artist and painter Makoto Fujimura can help us grasp the beauty that awaits us. He uses gold, in leaf and powder form, in his Nihonga paintings. Describing the nature of gold, he points out that most pure gold is nearly transparent and casts a bluish light, much like the description of the city-bride in Revelation. This description of the new Jerusalem inspired his work *Twin Rivers of Tamagawa*, in which he used the best gold possible as a symbol of the city of God descending into our world, transforming heaven and earth. Canadian artist Rachelle Kearns also used gold flake, with a very different technique, to create her painting *A New Land*. Brilliant white meets undulating golden lines, triggering the imagination to conceive the beauty of a new world. Commenting on the piece Kearns writes, "It is meant to ignite the imagination for what one day could be something far greater than what we have known—something so awesome, so beautiful, that it points us to Beauty itself."

John describes the whole city as having "the glory of God." This brilliant picture of Zion is a symbolic vision of our glorified beauty in the new heavens and earth, a beauty purchased by the sufferings of Christ. In our struggles with image and aging, we would do well to remember how God sees us—as beautiful as his own gleaming white bride, the very city of God!

BEAUTY SOOTHES SUFFERING

At the end of the miniseries *The Band of Brothers,* citizens and soldiers are surrounded by rubble in a derelict city. Gloom hangs in the air. Then some raggedy musicians gather up their instruments and start to play Beethoven's sixth symphony. The atmosphere begins to shift. Sonic beauty lifts spirits, hinting at the hope of a brighter future. Like the original recipients of John's letter, this beatific vision is given to lift the spirits of those who suffer in this world.

Beauty soothes suffering because it carries the promise of wholeness and restoration. When I was shuffling around the nurses' station trying to recover from surgery, I would pass framed photographs of flowers, trees, and mountains. As I did, my spirits lifted, sensing that restoration was possible. Whenever suffering hits, consider the comfort that comes from a vision of beauty. You might attend a classical concert, tour a museum, go for a hike, or best of all, meditate on your magnificent future described in Revelation 21–22. Lift your eyes from the momentary afflictions and look to Christ, and your troubles will gradually be eclipsed by the eternal weight of glory. Behold Christ more than your sufferings and his beauty will become your beauty. Beauty soothes suffering because it reminds us, in the midst of despair, that true beauty remains. Wholeness is coming and Christ with it. The image of the bride also reminds us of the people who need the beauty of Zion, the goodness of Christ, and the truth of the Spirit.

The reward of Zion is for those who overcome, persevere, and fight for the fruit of the Spirit. Putting to death the deeds of the flesh by the Spirit, we live. To those who contend for faith in the risen Christ, their faith will become sight—blazing glory, fiery eyes, hair like white wool, feet like burnished bronze, the voice of many waters, his face shining like the sun. Jesus is terrifyingly beautiful. Witnessing this vision, John falls to his feet as though dead, but Jesus lays a hand on him and says, "Fear not, I am the first and the last, and the living one. I died, and behold I am alive forevermore" (Rev 1:17-18). Jesus possesses a beauty so great, so strong, it sends shivers down the spine. But he also possesses a beauty that lifts us up. In the lyrics of David Ramirez:

> You have a beauty like no other
> And a confidence that brings me fear
> If I compare myself too long I might just run away
> But you have a grace that keeps me here.

This is the Lord Jesus—beautiful and strong, terrifying and soothing, full of the grace that keeps us near. If we keep our eyes on him, we *will* overcome.

FINAL WORD

The most meaningful, creative, satisfying life possible is the one lived here in Spirit. The Spirit has given us a foretaste of the future and longs for us to extend that taste to this world. Even after the Spirit has transformed all things, we will continue to live here, in a renewed heavens and earth, because of his sustaining, life-generating presence. With the creation project complete, the Spirit will commence his work through us in a new creation project, wilder and more satisfying than anything we can imagine. This should bring us to the point of worship, expressed in the virtuous fruit we bear and the culture we create. We will forever worship the Almighty in soul-gladdening praise because he gave his Son, Jesus Christ, to die and rise for our sins—the very same Jesus who is the beginning and the end, the king of all creation, who sits on the throne of the city to come and will forever illuminate the cosmos with his celestial glory. Surely he is worthy of our praise, together with the Father and the Spirit: Glory be to the Father, and to the Son, and to the Holy Spirit. As it was in the beginning, is now and will be forever. Amen.

The Spirit and the saints who have finished their race call us toward this transformed future: "The Spirit and the Bride say, 'Come.' And let the one who hears say, 'Come'" (Rev 22:17).

Acknowledgments

I AM INDEBTED TO Professor Richard Lovelace, whose teaching and writing gave me a vision of full-bodied Christian faith. Professor Colin Gunton, through his books, and Sean McDonough, through his teaching, helped me ground that vision in a robust trinitarian doctrine of creation. Each of them emphasized the person and work of the Holy Spirit in a way that changed my life. I'll never forget Sean's comment, "Who do you think is behind 'common grace'?—the Holy Spirit."

InterVarsity Press was just fantastic to work with on this project. I'm also grateful to my dear friend, Stephen Witmer, who read through a draft of this book and gave me thoughtful feedback and encouragement. My wife, Robie, advocated for this book for years. Thank you for your patience, constant belief, and encouragement, Honey.

Finally, I thank God—Father, Son, and Holy Spirit—for conceiving of a universe in which truth, beauty, and goodness are real, and meaning, creativity, and satisfaction are possible, and placing me in it.

Discussion Questions

1 THE GREATEST GIFT

1. How would you describe your relationship with the Holy Spirit?
2. How could your response to miraculous gifts distort your relationship with the Spirit?
3. What does the author mean by saying the most meaningful, creative, satisfying life is lived here in Spirit?
4. Which aspect do you want more of: meaning, creativity, or satisfaction?

2 CULTURE WITH THE SPIRIT

1. How can you relate to the idea of wanting to take in creation or do something with it? Why do you feel that way?
2. Did you learn something new about the Holy Spirit in this chapter?
3. What is culture? How does the Spirit relate to culture?
4. What would it look like for you to better bear God's image?
5. What cultural stewardship has God entrusted to you? How is the Spirit prompting you to change your approach to culture?

3 MORE THAN A FORCE

1. What do you find challenging about knowing the Holy Spirit?
2. Which of his attributes caught your attention? How can you respond to this observation?
3. Which of the Spirit's actions surprised you? Look up the corresponding Scriptures and reflect on how you might rely on the Spirit in a fresh way.
4. Do you worship the Spirit? Why or why not?

4 RENEWING ALL THINGS

1. How does our preoccupation with accomplishing prevent us from hearing the Spirit's voice?

2. What can you learn from the story of Elijah and his encounter with the small, still voice?

3. What steps can you take to cultivate more periods of silence so you can hear the voice of the Spirit?

4. Of the three recommended ways to listen to God's voice in Scripture, which one do you need to put into practice? What will you do to implement it?

5 THE SPIRIT OF SILENCE

1. Why are we incongruent with God? How does the Spirit reconcile this incongruence?

2. What is "new" about new life in the Spirit? How can that newness find greater expression in your life?

3. What difference does union with Christ make when you're facing anxiety?

4. Pick another gospel metaphor and meditate on how the Spirit works through it. What did you learn about the Spirit?

5. How might the Spirit's cosmic work in new creation influence your everyday life?

6 MORE THAN CONVIVIALITY

1. What is the difference between conviviality and community? How have you confused the two? Do you need to change your expectations of community as a result?

2. How does the Spirit alter your relationships?

3. Is the Spirit prompting you to forgive someone in particular? What steps might you need to take to reconcile with them?

4. How can you follow the Spirit through crisis? What might he be teaching you in your pain?

7 THE GREAT COMPANION

1. How might the Spirit be prompting you to cross the invisible line between church and the world?

2. Where do you see impatience with results in your life? What steps can you take to cultivate the patience of willing something eternal?

3. Where do you see opportunity, need, and desire converging for you to express mercy or advocate for justice?

4. Do you need to adjust your expectations of the Spirit's pace in order to see him work?

8 DISCERNING PROMPTINGS

1. Can you think of a time when you really wished you had a friend who wouldn't disappoint you? Imagine how your response would have been different if you replaced the fictional friend with the actual Helper.

2. How can you cultivate deeper companionship with the Spirit?

3. What truth is the Spirit calling you to trust more?

4. How does the Spirit help us when we fail to stand for what's true?

9 PRAYING IN THE SPIRIT

1. Do you lean toward ignoring the Spirit or projecting your desires onto him?

2. Which of the three tests of discernment do you need to practice more often to better hear the Spirit?

3. Do you make too much or too little of the Spirit's prophetic role? What do you need to adjust, through study and practice, to better honor the Holy Spirit's promptings?

4. How can you better value the infallible voice of the Spirit in Scripture?

10 MISSION WITH THE WIND

1. Should we pray to the Holy Spirit? Why or why not?

2. Which of the "praying in" pitfalls do you tend to fall into? How can you better avoid those to enjoy prayer more?

3. What would it look like for your prayers to go for a walk?

11 EXPERIENCING THE POWER

1. Since the Spirit is a person, should we be less concerned with him as a power?

2. Describe Jesus' relationship with the Holy Spirit. What stands out?

3. What does it mean to be filled with the Holy Spirit?

4. Which alternative power supplies are you tempted to rely on most? How can you repent of those and rely on the Holy Spirit instead?

12 THE SHAPE OF SUFFERING

1. Can you think of a time of suffering where the Spirit's presence made a difference? How does his omnipresence hold promise for hard times?

2. How did the Spirit help Jesus through his suffering? How can this help you?

3. Why is the Spirit described as eternal in Hebrews 9:14? How does his eternal work elevate your view of Jesus and secure your place with him?

13 BEARING FRUIT

1. How can you identify with boredom in the Christian life? How does Scripture speak to that?

2. Can you relate to the battle between your smartphone and God? What can you do to let the Spirit win out and be more present with others?

3. How does the Spirit offer a greater identity than being in the know or connected?

4. What are some ordinary ways you can better yield to the Spirit's promptings to bear his fruit? Which aspects of the fruit of the Spirit is he calling your attention to?

5. What obstacles do you need to overcome to respond to the Spirit's prompt to pray on the spot for others?

14 THE FUTURE OF THE SPIRIT

1. What will the Spirit do in heaven?

2. How does God want you to respond to Scripture's description of judgment and renewal? What does the Spirit do for his people during this time?

3. If the future is a teeming city, how should that affect your work and hobbies now?

4. If the future is a beautiful bride, how do you need to adjust your self-image or notions of beauty? How can you bring more beauty into the present?

5. How can this chapter change the way you worship?

Recommended Reading

The Holy Spirit, Sinclair B. Ferguson. A solid introduction to a theology of the Spirit.

The Holy Spirit in Mission, Gary Tyra. Emphasizes the Spirit's prophetic work through the church, in speech and action, for the mission of God.

Knowing the Holy Spirit Through the Old Testament, Christopher J. H. Wright. In this brief book Wright does a great job explaining who the Spirit is in the Old Testament and how that relates to our New Testament experience.

Practicing the Power, Sam Storms. A balanced book on the miraculous gifts of the Spirit. You may not agree with everything but will find it challenging and helpful.

The Spirit-Filled Church, Terry Virgo. This book by a veteran church and organizational leader contains a lot of wisdom for Spirit-filled living. The chapters on leadership and prayer are excellent.

Notes

1 THE GREATEST GIFT

p. 6   *Man, sub-creator*: J. R. R. Tolkien, "On Fairy Stories," available at www.excellence-in-literature.com/wp-content/uploads/2013/10 /fairystoriesbytolkien.pdf.

p. 8   *Signal of transcendence*: Peter Berger, *A Rumor of Angels: Modern Society and the Rediscovery of the Supernatural* (New York: Anchor Books, 1969), 60.

2 CULTURE WITH THE SPIRIT

p. 12   *Culture is what we make*: Ken Myers develops this idea in his excellent book *All God's Children and Blue Suede Shoes* (Wheaton, IL: Crossway, 1989).

      In 1936 a young engineer: Daniel Engber, "Who Made That Ski Lift?," *New York Times Magazine*, February 21, 2014, www.nytimes .com/2014/02/23/magazine/who-made-that-ski-lift.html.

p. 13   *Two hands*: Irenaeus of Lyons, *Against the Heresies*, ed. Alexander Roberts and James Donaldson, The Apostolic Fathers with Justin Martyr and Irenaeus (Grand Rapids: Eerdmans, 2002), 4.pref.1; 4.20.1; 4.33.4; 5.1.3; 5.5.1; 5.6.1; 5.17.4; 5.28.4; 5.35.2.

      It was not angels: Irenaeus, *Against the Heresies*, 4.20.1.

p. 14   *The universe itself owes*: Christopher J. H. Wright, *Knowing the Holy Spirit Through the Old Testament* (Downers Grove, IL: IVP Academic, 2006), 34.

p. 16   *Bethink thee first:* Basil, *On the Holy Spirit*, 16.38, in *Nicene and Post-Nicene Fathers*, ed. Philip Schaff, www.ccel.org/ccel/schaff /npnf208.vii.xvii.html.

p. 19   *Our work can contribute:* To read more about this vision of work and how to work for human flourishing, check out Amy Sherman, *Kingdom Calling: Vocational Stewardship for the Common Good* (Downers Grove, IL: InterVarsity Press, 2011).

         I think that one of the things: Quoted in Ian Parker, "The Shape of Things to Come," *New Yorker*, February 23, 2012, www.newyorker .com/magazine/2015/02/23/shape-things-come.

p. 20   *To find work that perfectly fits:* Os Guinness, *The Call: Finding and Fulfilling the Central Purpose of Your Life* (Nashville: Thomas Nelson, 2003), 50.

         Creation is a project: Colin E. Gunton, *The Triune Creator: A Historical and Systematic Study* (Grand Rapids: Eerdmans, 1998), 197.

3 MORE THAN A FORCE

p. 21   *Million Dollar Baby:* Directed by Clint Eastwood, screenplay by Paul Haggis (Warner Bros., 2004).

p. 22   *Faith must seek understanding:* Augustine, *On the Trinity*, 1.1. Edmund Hill points this out in his introduction to Saint Augustine, *The Trinity* (Hyde Park, NY: New City Press, 1991), 22.

p. 27   *About sixty percent:* Bob Smeitana, "Americans Believe in Heaven, Hell, and a Little Bit of Heresy," Lifeway Research, October 28, 2014, www.lifewayresearch.com/2014/10/28/americans-believe-in -heaven-hell-and-a-little-bit-of-heresy.

4 RENEWING ALL THINGS

p. 31   *In the OASIS, you can become:* Ernest Cline, *Ready Player One* (New York: Crown Publishing, 2011), 57.

p. 32   *Actually, our self-perception:* Paul Tripp, *Dangerous Calling: Confronting the Unique Challenges of Pastoral Ministry* (Wheaton, IL: Crossway, 2015), 152.

p. 34   *A holy spirit wafting:* Ann Powers, "Review: Alison Krauss, 'Windy City,'" First Listen, February 9, 2017, www.npr.org/2017/02/09 /514096051/first-listen-alison-krauss-windy-city.

         A holy spirit indwells: Quoted in Craig Keener, *The Mind of the Spirit: Paul's Approach to Transformed Thinking* (Grand Rapids: Baker Books, 2016), 130.

p. 35 *Union with Christ*: See Jonathan K. Dodson, *The Unbelievable Gospel: Say Something Worth Believing* (Grand Rapids: Zondervan, 2015), 123-31.

5 THE SPIRIT OF SILENCE

p. 44 *Let us never deceive*: Søren Kierkegaard, *Purity of Heart Is to Will One Thing*, ed. and trans. Howard V. Hong and Edna H. Hong, Kierkegaard's Writings 15 (Princeton, NJ: Princeton University Press, 1993), 92.

p. 45 *A thin sound*: Alternatively, some scholars translate this whisper as a "roaring, thunderous sound" or a "thunderous voice." Yet Elijah demonstrates very little fear of God, speaking plainly of his accomplishments before the Lord. See Jeffrey Niehaus, *God at Sinai* (Grand Rapids: Zondervan, 1995), 248.

p. 46 *If Bible study married prayer*: Tim Keller, "Adoring Christ: Communion with God," lecture, Preaching Christ in a Postmodern World, September 10, 2008, itunes.apple.com/us/itunes-u/preaching-christ-in -postmodern/id378879885.

p. 49 *God speaks so we can*: John Frame, *The Doctrine of the Word of God* (Philadelphia: P&R, 2010), 3.

p. 50 *We are listening*: Jeremy Quillo, "We Are Listening," *Before the Throne* (Louisville, KY: Sojourn Music, 2006), sojournchurch.com /wp-content/uploads/2014/10/We-Are-Listening.pdf.

6 MORE THAN CONVIVIALITY

p. 53 *In the wind of the storm*: Jeffrey Niehaus, *God at Sinai* (Grand Rapids: Zondervan, 1995), 157.

These wind and fire scenes: I owe Dr. Meredith Kline a great debt for opening my eyes to the presence of the Spirit in Scripture. For further analysis of these images see Meredith Kline, *Images of the Spirit* (Eugene, OR: Wipf & Stock, 1998).

p. 55 *We're not far away*: Ray Bradbury, *Fahrenheit 451* (New York: Ballantine Books, 1953).

p. 56 *Now, the signals we send*: Arcade Fire, "Reflektor," *Reflektor* (New York: Arcade Fire Music, 2013).

p. 59 *It can be so hard*: Aldous Harding, "Imagining My Man," *Party* (London: 4AD, 2017).

Pain is our mother: Over the Rhine, "Nobody Number One," *Ohio* (Milwaukee, WI: Back Porch, 2003).

7 THE GREAT COMPANION

p. 61   *All of this [is] like some ancient*: Cormac McCarthy, *The Road* (New York: Vintage, 2007), 74.

p. 63   *This failure to recognize*: Richard Lovelace, *Dynamics of Spiritual Life: An Evangelical Theology of Renewal* (Downers Grove, IL: IVP Academic, 1979), 130.

p. 64   *The Spirit must stop being merely*: Edward W. Klink, *John: An Exegetical Commentary* (Grand Rapids: Zondervan, 2016), 645.

attempts to conceive of the Holy Spirit: Regarding the universal spirit, see Rhonda Byrne, *The Secret* (Hillsborough, OR: Atria Books, 2006), and about the so-called "infinite spirit," see most recently Ellen Tadd, *The Infinite View: A Guidebook to Life on Earth* (New York: TarcherPerigee, 2017).

One who is called to someone's aid: "Parakletos," *A Greek-English Lexicon of the New Testament and Other Early Christian Literature*, ed. Walter Bauer et al., 3rd ed. (Chicago: University of Chicago Press, 2000), 766.

p. 65   *Over a million Christians were killed*: Todd M. Johnson, ed., *World Christian Database* (Boston: Brill, 2014).

p. 69   *You are not in fact supposed to see*: J. I. Packer, *Keeping in Step with the Spirit* (Wheaton, IL: Revel, 1984), 66.

p. 70   *The principle aim of the Spirit*: Sam Storms, *Practicing the Power: Welcoming the Gifts of the Holy Spirit in Your Life* (Grand Rapids: Zondervan, 2017), 183.

8 DISCERNING PROMPTINGS

p. 76   *There are various views*: See Stan Gundry & Wayne Grudem, eds., *Are Miraculous Gifts for Today? 4 Views* (Grand Rapids: Zondervan, 2005). See also *ESV Study Bible: The Holy Bible English Standard Version* (Wheaton, IL: Crossway, 2011), 2209, and Sam Storms, *Practicing the Power: Welcoming the Gifts of the Holy Spirit in Your Life* (Grand Rapids: Zondervan, 2017), 82-146.

The first view sees prophecy: For more on this view, see Wayne Grudem, *The Gift of Prophecy in the New Testament and Today* (Wheaton, IL: Crossway, 1998), 313.

9 PRAYING IN THE SPIRIT

p. 82   *I mean, it is just strange*: John Piper, "Should I Pray to the Father, the Son, or the Spirit?," Desiring God, August 29, 2014, www.desiringgod .org/interviews/should-i-pray-to-the-father-the-son-or-the-spirit.

p. 82 *Come, Creator Spirit*: Stanley Hauerwas and William Willimon, *The Holy Spirit* (Nashville: Abingdon Press, 2015), 8.

Breathe in me, O Holy Spirit: This prayer is commonly attributed to Augustine, though the original source is unknown.

p. 83 *The promise of bestowing*: John Owen, *The Holy Spirit*, The Works of John Owen, vol. 3, ed. William H. Goold (1850–1853; repr., Carlisle, PA: Banner of Truth, 2000), 155, emphasis added.

p. 86 *Intensifies the petition*: Cited in Anthony C. Thiselton, *The Holy Spirit Through the Centuries* (Grand Rapids: Eerdmans, 2013), 186.

p. 87 *Praying in the Spirit is not only*: Gordon Fee, *God's Empowering Presence: The Holy Spirit in the Letters of Paul* (Peabody, MA: Hendrickson, 1994), 732.

Let your thoughts take you: Cited in Timothy Keller, *Prayer: Experiencing Awe and Intimacy with God* (New York: Penguin, 2014), 251.

10 MISSION WITH THE WIND

p. 92 *Whatever it is, we need to*: For an excellent treatment of the Spirit's work in the mission of the church see Gary Tyra, *The Holy Spirit in Mission: Prophetic Speech and Action in Christian Witness* (Downers Grove, IL: IVP Academic, 2011).

p. 94 *I could recount many more*: I share some of these in Jonathan Dodson, *The Unbelievable Gospel: Say Something Worth Believing* (Grand Rapids: Zondervan, 2015), 143-89.

p. 95 *Meeting needs through deeds*: Timothy Keller, *Ministries of Mercy* (Phillipsburg, NJ: P&R, 1997).

11 EXPERIENCING THE POWER

p. 99 *When Bill Maris, founder of Google Ventures*: This story appears in Tad Friend, "Silicon Valley's Quest to Live Forever," *New Yorker*, April 3, 2017, www.newyorker.com/magazine/2017/04/03/silicon-valleys-quest-to-live-forever.

p. 100 *Faith-based tech*: This phrase is borrowed from Don DeLillo, *Zero K: A Novel* (New York: Scribner, 2016), which in some ways explores the implications of life lived in hope of scientific salvation.

The life of man consists: Irenaeus of Lyons, *Against the Heresies*, ed. Alexander Roberts and James Donaldson (Grand Rapids: Eerdmans, 2002), 4.34.5-7.

p. 101 *Reminiscent of the Spirit's hovering*: Sinclair Ferguson, *The Holy Spirit*, Contours of Christian Theology (Downers Grove, IL: IVP Academic, 1996), 38-40.

p. 102 *What could the Spirit of God contribute*: Bruce A. Ware, *The Man Christ Jesus: Theological Reflections on the Humanity of Christ* (Wheaton, IL: Crossway, 2013), 34.

p. 109 *Inception*: Written and directed by Christopher Nolan (Warner Bros., 2010).

p. 111 *One thing I find attractive*: Tim and Kathy Keller, *The Meaning of Marriage*, DVD series (Grand Rapids: Zondervan, 2015).

Best way to a customer's heart: Joseph Pine and James Gillmore, *The Experience Economy* (Boston: Harvard Business Review, 2011).

In craft beer, it's not just about: Eric Gorski, "Colorado Breweries Expand Beyond Tastings to Engage with Customers," *Denver Post*, February 24, 2017, www.denverpost.com/2017/02/24/colorado -breweries-expand-tastings.

p. 113 *The secular liturgy of the experience economy*: For more on the power of secular liturgies, see James K. A. Smith, *You Are What You Love* (Grand Rapids: Brazos Press, 2016), 27-55.

12 THE SHAPE OF SUFFERING

p. 118 *It was the power of the eternal*: Paul Ellingworth, *The Epistle to the Hebrews: A Commentary on the Greek Text* (Grand Rapids: Eerdmans, 1993), 457.

13 BEARING FRUIT

p. 124 *Relaxed*: Dallas Willard's answer is recounted in Alan Fadling, *An Unhurried Life: Following Jesus' Rhythms of Work and Rest* (Downers Grove, IL: InterVarsity Press, 2013), 8-9.

p. 126 *We should make a deliberate effort*: Richard Lovelace, *Dynamics of Spiritual Life: An Evangelical Theology of Renewal* (Downers Grove, IL: IVP Academic, 1979), 131.

p. 129 *The mediatorial elite*: I've searched for this article numerous times but have been unable to track it down. It might have been in *Mission Frontiers*, but I've unable to locate it.

p. 130 *The fallen human personality*: Lovelace, *Dynamics of Spiritual Life*, 89.

This fruit cannot be bought: Mark Sayers, *Strange Days: Life in the Spirit in a Time of Upheaval* (Chicago: Moody Press, 2017), 171.

p. 131   *If each, I told myself:* Robert Louis Stevenson, *The Strange Case of Dr. Jekyll and Mr. Hyde* (Roslyn, NY: Dover, 1991), 43.

p. 133   *One of John's favorite phrases:* David F. Ford, *The Drama of Life: Becoming Wise in the Spirit,* Kindle ed. (Grand Rapids: Brazos Press, 2015), loc. 456.

A habitual vision of greatness: Cited in John Piper, *The Hidden Smile of God* (Wheaton, IL: Crossway, 2001), 153.

14 THE FUTURE OF THE SPIRIT

p. 137   *It was a special pleasure:* Ray Bradbury, *Fahrenheit 451* (New York: Ballantine Books, 1953; repr., 2008), 3.

p. 138   *An hour of TV class:* Bradbury, *Fahrenheit 451*, 29.

Publicly disavowed: Bill Chappell, "Boy Says He Didn't Go to Heaven; Publisher Says It Will Pull Book," *The Two-Way,* January 15, 2015, www.npr.org/sections/thetwo-way/2015/01/15/377589757/boy -says-he-didn-t-go-to-heaven-publisher-says-it-will-pull-book.

p. 140   *God threatens terrible things:* Jeremy Taylor (1613–1667), "Christ's Advent to Judgment," The World's Great Sermons, www.authorama .com/worlds-great-sermons-3.html.

p. 141   *The number seven is also used:* Richard Bauckham, *The Theology of the Book of Revelation* (Cambridge: Cambridge University Press, 1993), 110.

Of the elements of the world: John Calvin, *Commentaries on the Catholic Epistles,* trans. and ed. John Owen, Christian Classics Ethereal Library, www.ccel.org/ccel/calvin/calcom45.vii.iv.iii.html.

p. 147   *Describing the nature of gold:* Makoto Fujimura, *Refractions: A Journey of Faith, Art, and Culture* (Colorado Springs, CO: NavPress, 2009), 21.

p. 148   *It is meant to ignite:* Quotation from a personal email from Rachelle Kearns, 2016. See her work at www.rachellekearns.com.

p. 149   *You have a beauty:* David Ramirez, "Fires," *American Soil* (David Ramirez, 2009), davidramirez.bandcamp.com/track/fires.

Scripture Index